New Directions for Institutional Research

John F. Ryan
EDITOR-IN-CHIEF

Gloria Crisp
ASSOCIATE EDITOR

New Scholarship in Critical Quantitative Research—Part 1: Studying Institutions and People in Context

Frances K. Stage
Ryan S. Wells

EDITORS

Number 158
Jossey-Bass
San Francisco

✳ 882105906

New Scholarship in Critical Quantitative Research—Part 1:
Studying Institutions and People in Context
Frances K. Stage and Ryan S. Wells (eds.)
New Directions for Institutional Research, no. 158
John F. Ryan, Editor-in-Chief
Gloria Crisp, Associate Editor

NEW DIRECTIONS FOR INSTITUTIONAL RESEARCH (ISSN 0271-0579, electronic ISSN 1536-075X) is part of The Jossey-Bass Higher and Adult Education Series and is published quarterly by Wiley Subscription Services, Inc., A Wiley Company, at Jossey-Bass, One Montgomery Street, Suite 1200, San Francisco, California 94104-4594 (publication number USPS 098-830). POSTMASTER: Send address changes to New Directions for Institutional Research, Jossey-Bass, One Montgomery Street, Suite 1200, San Francisco, California 94104-4594.

INDIVIDUAL SUBSCRIPTION RATE (in USD): $89 per year US/Can/Mex, $113 rest of world; institutional subscription rate: $317 US, $357 Can/Mex, $391 rest of world. Single copy rate: $29. Electronic only–all regions: $89 individual, $317 institutional; Print & Electronic–US: $98 individual, $365 institutional; Print & Electronic–Canada/Mexico: $98 individual, $405 institutional; Print & Electronic–Rest of World: $122 individual, $439 institutional.

EDITORIAL CORRESPONDENCE should be sent to John F. Ryan at jfryan@uvm.edu.

New Directions for Institutional Research is indexed in *Academic Search* (EBSCO), *Academic Search Elite* (EBSCO), *Academic Search Premier* (EBSCO), *CIJE: Current Index to Journals in Education* (ERIC), *Contents Pages in Education* (T&F), *EBSCO Professional Development Collection* (EBSCO), *Educational Research Abstracts Online* (T&F), *ERIC Database* (Education Resources Information Center), *Higher Education Abstracts* (Claremont Graduate University), *Multicultural Education Abstracts* (T&F), *Sociology of Education Abstracts* (T&F).

Microfilm copies of issues and chapters are available in 16mm and 35mm, as well as microfiche in 105mm, through University Microfilms, Inc., 300 North Zeeb Road, Ann Arbor, Michigan 48106-1346.

www.josseybass.com

THE ASSOCIATION FOR INSTITUTIONAL RESEARCH (AIR) is the world's largest professional association for institutional researchers. The organization provides educational resources, best practices, and professional development opportunities for more than 4,000 members. Its primary purpose is to support members in the process of collecting, analyzing, and converting data into information that supports decision making in higher education.

CONTENTS

This chapter briefly traces the development of the concept of critical quantitative inquiry, provides an expanded conceptualization of the tasks of critical quantitative research, offers theoretical explanation and justification for critical research using quantitative methods, and previews the work of quantitative criticalists presented in this volume.

Critical Quantitative Inquiry in Context

Frances K. Stage, Ryan S. Wells

Seven years ago, *New Directions for Institutional Research* published the volume, *Using Quantitative Data to Answer Critical Questions* (Stage, 2007). In that volume, a group of quantitative researchers sought to differentiate their approaches to quantitative research from more traditional positivistic and postpositivistic approaches. The term *quantitative criticalist* was used to describe a researcher who used quantitative methods to represent educational processes and outcomes to reveal inequities and to identify perpetuation of those that were systematic. The term also included researchers who question models, measures, and analytical practices, in order to ensure equity when describing educational experiences. These scholars resisted *traditional* quantitative research motivations that sought solely to confirm theory and explain processes.

In this chapter, we briefly summarize the academic basis of the underlying constructs related to critical quantitative inquiry, describe critiques of this perspective, and provide an overview of the work of the quantitative criticalists highlighted in this volume. Next, we discuss the future of the critical quantitative paradigm in two ways: (a) an expanded conceptualization of the tasks of critical quantitative inquiry regarding oppression and underrepresentation of particular groups of people, and (b) continued scrutiny and reflection on the theoretical underpinnings of critical quantitative research as it moves forward.

Background

The academic relationship between qualitative and quantitative researchers had evolved from mutual disdain in the 1980s, characterized by paradigm debates at academic meetings and in journals, to an uncomfortable truce

NEW DIRECTIONS FOR INSTITUTIONAL RESEARCH, no. 158 © 2014 Wiley Periodicals, Inc.
Published online in Wiley Online Library (wileyonlinelibrary.com) • DOI: 10.1002/ir.20041

through the 1990s, simply ignoring one another's scholarship but competing fiercely regarding grants, awards, and hires based on methodological issues. As quantitative criticalist scholars, my colleagues and I wanted more, and sought a *rapprochement*, believing that any scholar could learn from critical research, no matter the method, including our own critical quantitative work. We resisted the term positivist with its implications of fixed theoretical frameworks and prescriptive variable definitions. We used quantitative work, not to *prove* the relevance of grand theories, but rather to add to knowledge about the students and faculty whom we studied, and specifically those who were underrepresented and/or oppressed.

Kincheloe and McLaren's (1994) description of critical work was useful to us as we attempted to describe our view of our own work:

- Thought is mediated by socially and historically created power relations.
- Facts cannot be isolated from values.
- The relationship between concept and object is never fixed and is often socially mediated.
- Language is central to the formation of subjectivity.
- Certain groups in society hold privilege over others that is maintained if subordinates accept their status as natural.
- Oppression has many faces that must be examined simultaneously.
- Mainstream research practices generally reproduce class, race, and gender oppression.

We acknowledged qualitative approaches as central in critical inquiry, but argued that quantitative approaches had a contribution to make beyond what had been known as traditional quantitative scholarly inquiry. We asserted that quantitative approaches should be employed in explicitly critical inquiry as well.

Evolving Critical Quantitative Inquiry

The chapters of the 2007 volume described the work of quantitative criticalist scholars who were engaged in one of two related, but differing tasks. The first was to "use data to represent educational processes and outcomes on a large scale to reveal inequities and to identify social or institutional perpetuation of systematic inequalities in such processes and outcomes," and the second was to "question the models, measures, and analytic practices of quantitative research in order to offer competing models, measures, and analytic practices that better describe the experiences of those who have not been adequately represented" (Stage, 2007, p. 10). The purpose of the volume was to encourage others to engage in similar sorts of quantitative criticalist work. To those tasks for critical quantitative researchers we now add a third, "to conduct culturally relevant research by studying institutions and people in context." Scholars engaged in such scholarship might delve more deeply into institutional contexts within which underrepresented scholars and students work and study.

Since publication of that first volume, growing numbers of researchers have embraced the term quantitative criticalist; some have written chapters for this volume. As such, these scholars have rejected the labels of positivist and postpositivist, and have turned their quantitative skills toward work on equity goals and outcomes. Encouragement of a critical quantitative perspective since the 2007 publication is also evident based on the existence of the ASHE Institutes on Equity and Critical Policy Analysis, one of which was titled "Research Methods for Critical Analysis of Quantitative Data." These institutes concluded with a special issue of *Review of Higher Education* where the observation was made, "the gap between critical policy studies and analysis and the development of a sustaining equity and access agenda remains large indeed" (Anderson, 2012, p. 135). The purpose of this volume is to extend the discussion of critical quantitative work, partially as it relates to the newly conceptualized third task, and to highlight recent higher education scholarship that employs the approach across a range of topics. Our hope is that this endeavor will not only raise awareness of past work but also encourage future research using a critical quantitative perspective that will help to shrink the gap between equity-minded research and policy.

Resistance to Quantitative Criticalism

Despite use among scholars such as those represented in this volume, and more acceptance in the higher education research community generally, those employing critical quantitative approaches have received criticism as well. On one side, this critique has come from critical qualitative researchers. One thrust of this critique seems to be that the epistemological underpinnings of quantitative research are fundamentally at odds with the goals of critical inquiry. However, Sprague (2005) points out that many of these criticisms—in her example from feminist research (but true of other critical research as well)—are really aimed at positivism more broadly. "That is, the critics are sliding from a concern about a particular *methodology* to a wholesale rejection of a class of *methods*" (p. 81).

Quantitative criticalists received a challenge in the original 2007 volume when Baez encouraged us to go beyond asking critical questions toward explicitly linking findings with suggested actions for social transformation. Many critical quantitative scholars do indeed provide suggestions for social transformation as well as changes in educational research methods; some of those prominent scholars include Estela Mara Bensimon and coauthors (Bensimon, Hao, & Bustillos, 2006), Sylvia Hurtado and coauthors (Hurtado, Alvarez, Guillermo-Wann, Cuellar, & Arellano, 2012), Edward St. John (2006), and Deborah Faye Carter (2006). Additionally, the newer scholars who wrote chapters for this volume advocate for changes in quantitative research methods as well as in educational practice.

Since that volume, others from the critical qualitative community have moved beyond such a challenge into an extended critique, arguing that a critical quantitative approach fails to represent fully a critical theoretical grounding because, while critical questions are important, to be truly critical the methods must be directly transformative and not rely on indirect action based on research results (Pasque, Carducci, Gildersleeve, & Kuntz, 2011). This deeper critique of the supposedly nontransformative nature of most critical quantitative work implies that no inquiry is critical that does not essentially employ some type of action research design. While we applaud critical research that precipitates action, quantitative and qualitative alike, we also value any research, no matter the method, that reveals inequity and unfairness in educational practice. While a healthy debate should continue concerning critical work, we believe that a wider conceptualization of critical inquiry has been, and will continue to be, both viable and valuable in the broad attempt to understand educational processes.

Less anticipated than critiques from qualitative researchers has been criticism from the dominant (positivist) quantitative perspective. These critiques either hold fast to the notion that there is an objective truth and reject critical notions of the existence of oppression and the need to address it, or presume that "bias exists but does not systematically favor particular social positions..." (Sprague, 2005, p. 83). In general, there seems to be a fear from this perspective that if you tamper with a positivist epistemology, the whole quantitative approach is somehow tainted. Interestingly, this criticism is similar to one of the main critiques from the qualitative side of the house, but in reverse, conflating methods and methodology.

Critiques described above have been partially manifested in resistance from faculty that is encountered by graduate students who attempt to make use of the critical quantitative paradigm. Additional resistance stems from journal editors and reviewers who critique researchers who explicitly use the paradigm. Among our own colleagues, we have seen dissertation committees reject the validity of this perspective, and journal reviewers recommend acceptance of a manuscript conditional on the removal of a section discussing the critical quantitative perspective.

We appreciate continued conversation about conducting rigorous and well-grounded research, and hope such concern about producing high-quality studies in higher education continues. However, questioning from a critical stance is an increasingly evident way of conducting quantitative research. This approach does not seek merely to verify models; it seeks new models and ways of measuring. Rather than focusing on explanation or fairness, the focus is on equity concerns that can be highlighted through analysis of large data sets and by examining differences by race, class, and gender. In this way, the products of the educational enterprise are explored to reveal systematic inequities that are produced within that enterprise for particular groups of people (Briscoe, 2008).

Summary of Chapters

The chapters that follow present work focused on underrepresented persons in a variety of levels of higher education. Each scholar has used critical quantitative approaches to examine access and success in the higher education arena. The scholarship described pushes the boundaries of what we know by questioning mainstream notions of higher education through the examination of policies, the reframing of theories and measures, and the reexamination of traditional questions for nontraditional populations. While the work is divergent, the commonality of the presentations lies in each scholar's critical approach to conventional quantitative scholarship via one or more of the three tasks outlined above. Their research is intended to highlight inequities as well as to explore factors not typically included in traditional quantitative analysis.

In Chapter 2, Williams studies students of color, examining how financial and academic barriers influence the efficacy of innovative pipeline interventions on STEM career-related plans for underrepresented students of color. Alcantar, in Chapter 3, examines researchers' use of a national data set to measure civic engagement and its relevance in models of college success for Latino students. She suggests alternate measures that are more relevant to the population. Next, Oseguera and Hwang investigate school context and other critical conditions for college access for low-income students by race and ethnicity in Chapter 4. They provide suggestions for policymakers and school administrators to improve academic preparation and college enrollment of low-income students.

In Chapter 5, Conway expands the critical quantitative perspective to examine degree completion and transfer for immigrants and children of immigrants. In Chapter 6, John and Stage examine the relative roles that minority-serving institutions, predominantly minority institutions, and predominantly White institutions play in the education of college students from U.S. underrepresented minority groups. Metcalf, in Chapter 7, takes a critical look at the transition to the STEM workforce. She interrogates the discourses, models, and data used when typically examining the STEM "pipeline" and complicates them with her analyses of underrepresented students. Finally, Rios-Aguilar, in Chapter 8, contextualizes the approaches of the authors in this volume within the general body of critical work in higher education. She provides an additional framework to support this type of research and provides suggestions for future research related to the topics of the individual chapters, as well as new directions for critical quantitative work more broadly.

Conclusion

Our expectation is that readers of this volume will gain an understanding of the usefulness of critical quantitative research to help understand the complex issues of access and success for underrepresented populations on college campuses. The research presented in the chapters that follow serve as exemplars for quantitative and critical work, while informing scholars interested in similar issues of access, success, and outcomes on college campuses. Hopefully, this work will inspire new possibilities for future research.

References

Anderson, G. M. (2012). Equity and critical policy analysis in higher education: A bridge still too far. *The Review of Higher Education, 36*(1), 133–142.

Baez, B. (2007). Thinking critically about the "critical": Quantitative research as social critique. In F. K. Stage (Ed.), *New Directions for Institutional Research: No. 133. Using quantitative data to answer critical questions* (pp. 17–23). San Francisco, CA: Jossey-Bass.

Bensimon, E. M., Hao, L., & Bustillos, L. T. (2006). Measuring the state of equity in public higher education. In P. Gandara, G. Orfield, & C. L. Horn (Eds.), *Expanding opportunity in higher education: Leveraging promise* (pp. 143–165). Albany: State University of New York Press.

Briscoe, K. (2008). *A response to using qualitative data to answer critical questions.* Unpublished manuscript, New York University, New York.

Carter, D. F. (2006). Key issues in the persistence of underrepresented minority students. In E. P. St. John & M. Wilkerson (Eds.), *New Directions for Institutional Research: No. 130. Reframing persistence research to improve academic success* (pp. 33–46). San Francisco, CA: Jossey-Bass.

Hurtado, S., Alvarez, C. L., Guillermo-Wann, C., Cuellar, M., & Arellano, L. (2012). A model for diverse learning environments: The scholarship on creating and assessing conditions for student success. In J. C. Smart & M. B. Paulsen (Eds.), *Higher education handbook of theory and research* (pp. 41–122). New York, NY: Springer.

Kincheloe, J. L., & McLaren, P. L. (1994). Rethinking critical theory and qualitative research. In N. Denzin & Y. Lincoln (Eds.), *Handbook of qualitative research* (pp. 138–157). London, UK: Sage Publications.

Pasque, P., Carducci, R., Gildersleeve, R. E., & Kuntz, A. M. (2011). Disrupting the ethical imperatives of "junior" critical qualitative scholars in the Era of Conservative Modernization. *Qualitative Inquiry, 17*(7), 571–588.

Sprague, J. (2005). *Feminist methodologies for critical researchers.* Walnut Creek, CA: Altamira Press.

Stage, F. K. (Ed.). (2007). *New Directions for Institutional Research: No. 133. Using quantitative data to answer critical questions.* San Francisco, CA: Jossey-Bass.

St. John, E. P. (2006). *Education and the public interest: Education reform, public finance, and access to higher education.* New York, NY: Springer.

FRANCES K. STAGE *is a professor of higher and postsecondary education in the Department of Administration, Leadership, and Technology at New York University.*

RYAN S. WELLS *is an assistant professor of higher education in the Department of Educational Policy, Research, and Administration at the University of Massachusetts Amherst.*

NEW DIRECTIONS FOR INSTITUTIONAL RESEARCH • DOI: 10.1002/ir

2

This chapter offers a critical lens for examining intervention efficacy. It highlights a conceptual framework particularly relevant for understanding the experiences of underrepresented students and illustrates how such framing can explicate the mechanisms that impede or enhance successful intervention outcomes in STEM fields.

Strains, Strengths, and Intervention Outcomes: A Critical Examination of Intervention Efficacy for Underrepresented Groups

Krystal L. Williams

There is a growing interest in better understanding the factors that influence the education pipeline from high school to higher education and competitive career fields for students from underrepresented groups (e.g., Greene & Winters, 2005; Perna, 2006). While the overall success rates for students in science, technology, engineering, and mathematics (STEM) fields are problematic, the success rates for various subgroups are even lower. For example, a report by the National Action Council for Minorities in Engineering, Inc. (2008) indicates that, in 2006, 68,000 engineering bachelor's degrees were awarded in the United States and only 8,500 of those were awarded to underrepresented students of color. There is also an issue regarding the gender gap in STEM fields. While women have earned a high percentage of bachelor's degrees in psychology since the early 1990s, they have been particularly underrepresented in other STEM fields such as engineering, physics, and computer science (Hill, Corbett, & St. Rose, 2010; National Science Foundation, 2013).

Issues concerning the STEM pipeline not only present challenges for students who are underrepresented in these fields, but also pose a potential threat for the future of America's economic competitiveness, and the sustainability of its 20th century position as one of the world's global powers (e.g., Bowman & St. John, 2011; National Research Council, 2009). To help address representation disparities in STEM fields, a number of interventions have been developed to facilitate students' success in these areas (Chubin, DePass, & Blockus, 2010; DePass & Chubin, 2009; Fagen & Labov, 2007;

NEW DIRECTIONS FOR INSTITUTIONAL RESEARCH, no. 158 © 2014 Wiley Periodicals, Inc.
Published online in Wiley Online Library (wileyonlinelibrary.com) • DOI: 10.1002/ir.20042

George, Neale, Van Horne, & Malcolm, 2001). However, we still have very little *theory-driven* knowledge about the various factors that influence intervention efficacy. While evaluation studies have suggested that these programs expand the pipeline in STEM, less is known about the factors that *impede* or *enhance* the success of various program participants. As a result, there is growing collaboration among several governmental agencies and nonprofits to support more comprehensive approaches to understanding and improving pipeline interventions that promote successful outcomes for underrepresented minorities and women in STEM fields (DePass & Chubin, 2009; Olson & Fagen, 2007).

Given this context, this chapter discusses a critical quantitative approach for understanding how to improve the efficacy of such pipeline interventions. It begins with a brief discussion of racial/ethnic and gender disparities in STEM. It then highlights the role of policy interventions in decreasing these gaps. Afterward, a strength-based framework for investigating intervention efficacy is outlined in detail. Finally, a theory-oriented evaluation is summarized which used this framework and interrogated a question that is currently beyond the reach of traditional evaluation research. This study explored intervention efficacy by investigating not *if* pipeline interventions "work," but *how* they operate for underrepresented students who often face both normative and nonnormative challenges in college. These challenges include adapting to strains related to their financial and academic background (e.g., financial hardships, academic preparation challenges, etc.), as well as overcoming structural barriers due to factors such as race and gender. The theory-oriented evaluation also highlighted how the multilevel cultural strengths that underrepresented students bring to intervention settings can also influence their outcomes in addition to barriers and strain. Overall, this research illustrates how quantitative data can be used to represent structural inequalities, educational processes, and outcomes for underrepresented students (Stage, 2007).

STEM Participation: Gender and Racial Disparities

There has been a growing focus on increasing student participation in STEM. Furthermore, there is a pressing need to decrease racial/ethnic and gender representation disparities in these fields. Men continue to outnumber women in many STEM areas, although the number of women in these fields is increasing. Underrepresentation issues continue even though a comparable number of women and men obtain the high school academic preparation necessary to pursue STEM majors in college (e.g., Hill et al., 2010). The gap in STEM majors between women and men is also reflected in gender differences among graduates in many science and engineering fields. Furthermore, the gap expands at the graduate level and in terms of representation in the STEM workforce (Beede et al., 2011).

NEW DIRECTIONS FOR INSTITUTIONAL RESEARCH • DOI: 10.1002/ir

There is an ongoing research agenda to determine the factors that contribute to the gender representation gap in many STEM fields. Some research suggests that environmental factors play a major role in the disparities that persists in college and beyond. A study by the American Association of University Women (AAUW; Hill et al., 2010) suggests that there is an implicit unconscious tendency to impose a gender orientation on certain fields with STEM being considered "male" and humanities "female." Also, the study indicates that women in "masculine" fields are assumed to be less competent and have to overcome gender bias in the work environment. However, when women are successful in these fields, they are perceived as less likeable (Hill et al., 2010). Each of these factors can have a deleterious effect on female representation in STEM.

Some minority groups are also underrepresented among STEM majors, graduates, and the resulting workforce (National Action Council for Minorities in Engineering, Inc., 2008). The reasons for this disparity are multifaceted. Despite popular opinion to the contrary, some research suggests that representation issues are not due to a lack of interest in the sciences among underrepresented students of color upon entering college (Anderson & Kim, 2006). Instead, inadequate precollege academic preparation is one important factor that limits these students' ability to pursue STEM majors (Anderson & Kim, 2006). Another is lower college persistence rate for underrepresented minorities in general and particularly in STEM fields (Alexander, Chen, & Grumbach, 2009; Anderson & Kim, 2006). These factors illustrate some of complexities underlying the representation challenge which must be accounted for in studies that seek to identify approaches for expanding underserved groups' opportunities in STEM.

STEM Participation and Policy Interventions

Given the need to establish a diverse pool of students in STEM, a number of policy initiatives have been developed to increase students' interest, participation, and educational advancement in these fields. For example, the White House Educate to Innovate Initiative was implemented to enhance the United States' national capacity in STEM. This initiative promotes STEM teaching improvements, partnerships with private sector, federal investment in STEM, and efforts to diversify these fields (White House, n.d.). Similarly, the Association for American Universities (AAU) Undergraduate STEM Education Initiative was launched to improve teaching and learning in STEM at AAU institutions (Association for American Universities, n.d.).

At the institutional level, many colleges and universities have developed interventions with similar ambitions to promote positive STEM outcomes—particularly future graduate work. While a litany of studies discuss factors that can exert a negative influence on college success such as affordability issues and limited prior academic exposure (e.g.,

Brazziel & Brazziel, 2001; DeBerard, Spielmans, & Julka, 2004; St. John, 2003, 2006; St. John, Fisher, Williams, & Daun-Barnett, 2008; St. John, Hu, & Fisher, 2011; St. John & Musoba, 2010), other research indicates that interventions can help to promote positive college outcomes directly and indirectly (e.g., Bauer & Bennett, 2003; Hunter, Laursen, & Seymour, 2006; Lopatto, 2004, 2007; Maton, Domingo, Stolle-McAllister, Zimmerman, & Hrabowski, 2009; Pender, Marcotte, Domingo, & Maton, 2010; Yauch, 2007). For example, the Meyerhoff Scholars Program is often discussed as an exemplary STEM intervention. This comprehensive program has been praised highly for increasing underrepresented minority students' participation in the sciences (e.g., Maton et al., 2009). Meyerhoff students are about five times more likely to have earned or be working toward a STEM PhD or MD/PhD than similar peers (Maton et al., 2009). Other research highlights positive STEM outcomes with regard to academic achievement, graduation rates, graduate school plans, and postbaccalaureate degree attainment for the Meyerhoff Scholars Program (Maton & Hrabowski, 2004; Maton, Hrabowski, & Schmitt, 2000; Maton, Pollard, McDougall Weise, & Hrabowski, 2012; Maton et al., 2009) and similar interventions (e.g., Bauer & Bennett, 2003; Russell, Hancock, & McCullough, 2007; Yauch, 2007). While some studies note that students' ambitions to attend graduate school are often shaped prior to program participation, the literature suggests that interventions can help to support or further these interests and to increase the likelihood of actual graduate school attendance (Lopatto, 2004, 2007; Russell et al., 2006, 2007; Yauch, 2007).

Intervention Efficacy Reexamined: A Strength-Based Approach

An expansive literature suggests that interventions can promote student success in STEM fields; however, our understanding of intervention efficacy needs further development. The Bowman Role Strain and Adaptation Model (BRSAM) is a strength-based framework that explains how interventions operate within a context of other important factors to influence successful outcomes in college and beyond (Figure 2.1). Bowman (2006) defines student role strain as the combination of objective difficulties that individuals face in their role as students, as well as the affiliated cognitive/subjective appraisal of those difficulties. Accordingly, the role strain construct includes the objective barriers that students face, as well as their resulting subjective responses to those objective challenges.

The BRSAM builds upon a growing body of literature that emphasizes the influence of student role strain, and multilevel strengths on successful education and career outcomes (e.g., Bandura, 1986; Robbins et al., 2004; Sedlacek, 2004). The framework employs a critical lens that helps to explicate underrepresented students' experiences in interventions. Toward this end, the model acknowledges not only the impact of interventions but also structural inequalities due to social stratification that can impede

Figure 2.1. A Strength-Based Model of Role Strain and Adaptation: Toward a Comprehensive Approach to Successful Student and Career Development

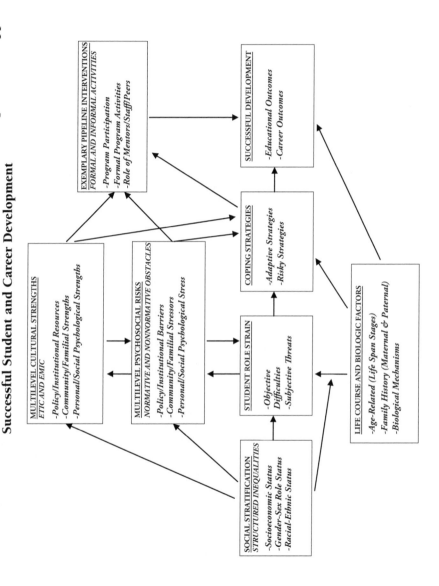

educational processes. The model notes that these inequalities can result in psychosocial obstacles, strain, and related risky coping strategies.

Because the BRSAM is a strength-based framework, in addition to obstacles to education and career success, it also highlights the multilevel strengths that underrepresented students have which can promote positive outcomes despite strains. Examples of these strengths include personal resiliency, as well as family and organizational support. Furthermore, the framework provides insight about other mechanisms that can facilitate intervention efficacy such as students adopting adaptive coping strategies in response to strain. Hence, the model expands current evaluative research by emphasizing factors that can enhance or impede intervention outcomes over and beyond the intervention experience, and investigating the mechanisms by which interventions promote successful educational and career outcomes—especially for underrepresented students. A deeper understanding of these issues will allow program administrators and stakeholders to develop and evaluate interventions that better serve the needs of underrepresented populations.

Evidence From the Field: Innovative Pipeline Interventions and STEM Career Plans

To illustrate the utility of the BRSAM, the following discussion outlines emerging findings from a study employing the role strain and adaptation framework to examine how underrepresented students' participation in pipeline interventions related to their advanced STEM career plans. This theory-driven study differs from traditional program evaluation research in that its primary objective is to better understand social psychological factors that can impede or enhance intervention participants' benefits, in contrast with a summative evaluation of overall intervention effects. With randomized experimental designs as the "gold standard," outcome evaluation studies examine the overall effects of an intervention and ask, "Does it work?" (Cook & Campbell, 1979; Hoyle, Harris, & Judd, 2002; Shadish, Cook, & Campbell, 2002). Theory-driven studies employ a range of different methods to explain underlying mechanisms and ask, "How and why does it work?" (e.g., Donaldson, 2007; Mark, Donaldson, & Campbell, 2011; Mark & Henry, 2004; Shadish, Cook, & Leviton, 1991). Such a theory-driven approach provides a deeper understanding of how student role strain and adaptation mechanisms influence intervention efficacy beyond the overall intervention effect. Furthermore, a more nuanced understanding of intervention outcomes has become a focal, policy-relevant issue for a number of national organizations including the National Institutes of Health, National Science Foundation, and the American Association for the Advancement of Science.

Using the BRSAM framework, the study employed policy-relevant indicators for student role strain, and culturally relevant measures for students' strengths. As a result, this research provided a holistic view of how barriers (objective and subjective) and adaptive strengths influence intervention efficacy. The overall study built upon an ongoing project, "Multi-Method Study of Exemplary Research Opportunity Interventions: Bridging Theory-Driven Research and Program Innovation," based at the University of Michigan National Center for Institutional Diversity and supported by the National Institutes of Health–National Institute for General Medical Sciences (1R01Gm088750-01).

Summer Research Opportunity Programs.   This study employed a rich set of survey data from the Committee on Institutional Cooperation (CIC) Summer Research Opportunities Program (SROP) to investigate the relationship between summer pipeline intervention participation and students' future plans to pursue a research career in STEM. The CIC SROP was initiated in 1986 and is currently active at each of the CIC institutions: Indiana University-Bloomington, the University of Illinois at Urbana-Champaign, the University of Iowa, the University of Michigan, Michigan State University, the University of Minnesota, Northwestern University, the Ohio State University, Pennsylvania State University, Purdue University, and the University of Wisconsin at Madison. The program is also active at the University of Illinois at Chicago and the University of Wisconsin at Milwaukee. Since its inception, the program has served over 9,000 students with the primary objective to increase the number of underrepresented students who attend graduate school and pursue research careers. The CIC SROP targets second- and third-year students who work with a faculty mentor during the summer for 8–10 weeks and reside on campus. Although CIC SROP is not an intervention for students in STEM fields exclusively, it has been awarded the prestigious Presidential Award for Excellence in Science, Mathematics, and Engineering Mentoring by the White House for successfully mentoring students in these fields (Committee on Institutional Cooperation, 2008). Seventy percent of the CIC SROP students in the study were STEM majors.

Students were surveyed at the beginning of the CIC SROP for summer 2011, during the fall term following the summer program, and after the first term of 2011–2012 academic year. Data were collected from program participants, as well as applicants who did not participate in the program, but had a similar summer research experience. Outcomes for these two groups were compared to a third group of applicants who had no research experience during the summer. Students in the intervention and comparison groups were similar on most key measures considered in the analysis.

Student Role Strain and Multilevel Strengths: The Use of Policy and Culturally Relevant Measures.   Previous evaluation research supports the overall positive influence of summer research program participation on various college outcomes (e.g., Bauer & Bennett, 2003; Hunter et al., 2006; Lopatto, 2004, 2007; Maton et al., 2009; Pender et al., 2010; Yauch, 2007). However, no existing study investigated how program participation relates to outcomes within the context of other important social and psychological factors. This framing provides a useful orientation for understanding underrepresented students' intervention experiences. The following discussion highlights the importance of employing these types of critical measures in quantitative research. More specifically, it illustrates how psychosocial factors, as represented by policy and culturally relevant measures, were employed in a theory-oriented evaluation of summer research programs.

In the study described, the BRSAM was employed to clarify how pipeline intervention participation relates to STEM research career plans, while also considering the strains and multilevel strengths that students from underrepresented groups bring to intervention settings. The outcome considered was students' plans to pursue research careers in STEM fields because of a policy interest in expanding opportunities in STEM research and faculty careers for underserved groups (National Action Council for Minorities in Engineering, Inc., 2008; National Science Foundation, 2013). Also, the research focused on strains in the financial and academic domains because of their policy relevance. Using a role strain and adaptation approach, this research considered both objective barriers and students' cognitive appraisals of those barriers. Such an approach acknowledged both the tangible barriers that underrepresented students have to overcome, as well as their subjective responses to those barriers. The objective measures included the use of public welfare programs, Pell grants, work study, and prior academic challenges as indicated by high school grade point average, and standardized test score. Students' subjective appraisals of objective barriers included financial stress, ability blame (i.e., attributing academic challenges to lack of ability), and academic discouragement.

In addition to financial and academic challenges, the study also examined how the negative relationship between these strains and the outcome might be mitigated by the strengths that students bring to intervention settings. In doing so, the study forwent a deficit orientation focused on strains in favor of a strength-based approach. Furthermore, while a number of studies focused on etic or universal strengths and college success (e.g., Zajacova, Lynch, & Espenshade, 2005), this research acknowledged the utility of emic or group-specific strengths. Accordingly, the analysis used measures for students' strengths that have particular relevance for underrepresented groups.

Students' strengths were considered at multiple levels. At the individual level, the study examined the relationship between personal resiliency and STEM research career plans. In other research, personal resiliency is often operationalized using etic (i.e., universal) measures with a particular emphasis on a general sense of mastery or self-efficacy (Bowman, 2013); however, this analysis utilized an emic (i.e., group-specific) measure of personal resiliency developed to have particular relevance for underrepresented students. *John Henryism* is defined as an "individual's self-perception that he can meet the demand of his environment through hard work and determination" (James, Hartnett, & Kalsbeek, 1983, p. 263). Although the measure was named after the legendary John Henry folklore to illustrate the psychosocial challenges that African Americans have to overcome in pursuit of success in different domains, its utility is not limited to this group. John Henryism is also applicable to other populations that confront similar structural barriers (James, 1994). Given that the program under study targets underrepresented students, this emic personal resiliency measure was appropriate for this analysis. Accordingly, the John Henryism measure was used to examine how students' perceptions about their ability to succeed in a given context relate to their STEM research career plans.

At the family level, this research also investigated how family support influenced underrepresented students' plans to pursue research careers using a culturally relevant measure. While other studies highlight the influence of parental support on various college outcomes, this study operationalized this construct with a measure of *extended family support*. Although Western tradition has normally defined family based on married heterosexual couples and their children living in the same household, many cultures define family in terms of both blood-kin and para-kin relationships (i.e., those who share familial-like bonds that may not be biologically based). This broader definition of family is often embraced by students from underrepresented groups (Reyes, 2002) and can be employed to examine how support from various family members relates to STEM research career plans. This approach recognizes the magnitude of influence that not only parents but also grandparents, mentors, and significant others can have on student success (e.g., Dennis, Phinney, & Chuateco, 2005).

A Comprehensive Examination of Role Strain, Strengths, and Intervention Outcomes

Multivariate regression was employed to investigate the relationship between intervention participation, role strain, multilevel strengths, and STEM research career plans, additively. Additionally, key product terms were examined for insight regarding how student strengths might moderate or mitigate strains. While a detailed discussion of the study is beyond the scope of this chapter, key findings are summarized to illustrate how a critical quantitative approach helps to explicate intervention outcomes for underrepresented students.

The evidence supports the conceptual guidance offered by the critical role strain and adaptation framework. The results suggest that understanding how intervention participation relates to students' plans to pursue research careers in STEM requires a more nuanced examination than what is generally offered by traditional evaluation studies. Despite the supports and exposure offered by intervention participation, students' strains remained a challenge and were negatively related to the outcome. For example, students with lower ACT scores had lower plans to pursue STEM research careers even after accounting for intervention participation. This suggests that students who come to an intervention with academic challenges may still have difficulties achieving certain outcomes despite their program experiences. It also suggests that interventions should consider strategies for reducing academic strain in order to increase intervention efficacy and to better promote the next generation of STEM researchers from underrepresented groups.

Aligned with the role strain and adaptation approach, it is also important to note the strengths that students can use to promote successful outcomes. In the analysis, emerging findings suggest that personal resiliency helped to mitigate the negative relationship between academic strain and STEM research career plans. From a practical perspective, this underscores the need for interventions not only to bolster students' academic preparation, but also to focus on enhancing students' noncognitive skills such as personal resiliency. Additionally, this finding offers critical quantitative insight regarding the appropriate use of measures. As an etic (i.e., universal) measure of resiliency, scholars who study self-efficacy suggest that general self-efficacy measures are limited in their ability to explain educational outcomes because students' *general* efficacy beliefs do not necessarily reflect their beliefs about their *academic* abilities. Accordingly, some literature suggests that domain-specific resiliency measures such as academic self-efficacy are more appropriate when studying educational outcomes (e.g., Zajacova et al., 2005). From a critical perspective, similar critiques can be made regarding the use of culturally relevant measures. The study suggests that emic (i.e., group-specific) resiliency measures can help to explain academic outcomes for underrepresented groups. This finding emphasizes the need to interrogate the measures used to explain the experiences of underrepresented populations in quantitative research. Also, this finding illustrates how the relationship between emic general personal resiliency and college success for underrepresented groups may differ from the relationship between etic general personal resiliency and success for other groups.

Lessons Learned: A Critical Assessment of Pipeline Interventions

This analysis employed a critical approach for assessing intervention efficacy by challenging questions that undergird traditional evaluation research and employing a more expansive framework to gain a deeper understanding of underrepresented students' experiences. In theory-oriented evaluation research, being critical requires the scholar to move beyond questions concerning whether interventions work to questions of how, why, and for whom. While traditional evaluation research is important, it is only the first step in a comprehensive study of interventions. Evaluations that only investigate whether interventions "work," in general, fail to interrogate the mechanisms through which such programs operate and are no longer sufficient or prudent from a policy perspective. To better serve underrepresented populations, it is important to know which factors impede and enhance students' outcomes, and to align future program development and evaluation accordingly.

Critical quantitative analysis not only requires reflection regarding the types of questions asked, but it also encourages reflection in terms of the data employed to answer those questions. The aforementioned study examined how objective financial and academic challenges can impede successful student outcomes. In addition, the research went a step further by acknowledging that students respond subjectively to objective challenges. As illustrated by the BRSAM, while the barriers themselves are important, a student makes subjective appraisals of those barriers and can respond to them with either risky or adaptive coping strategies. Acknowledging the objective challenges alone denies the complexity of how individuals respond to adversity.

Finally, the outlined study utilized culturally relevant measures for a more penetrating examination of student strengths. While etic (i.e., universal) measures provide useful insight about students' experiences generally, emic (i.e., group-specific) measures are better suited to represent underrepresented students experiences. Overall, this type of critical examination of pipeline interventions allows researchers to investigate intervention efficacy in a way that better acknowledges underrepresented students' experiences within interventions. From a practical perspective, this approach provides policy-relevant information about how to better serve students who have been traditionally underrepresented in STEM areas.

References

Alexander, C., Chen, E., & Grumbach, K. (2009). How leaky is the health career pipeline? Minority student achievement in college gateway courses. *Academic Medicine, 84*, 797–802.

Anderson, E., & Kim, D. (2006). *Increasing the success of minority students in science and technology*. Washington, DC: American Council on Education.

Association for American Universities. (n.d.). *AAU undergraduate STEM education initiative*. Retrieved from http://www.aau.edu/policy/article.aspx?id=12588

Bandura, A. (1986). *Social foundations of thought and action: A social cognitive theory*. Englewood Cliffs, NJ: Prentice-Hall.

Bauer, K., & Bennett, J. (2003). Alumni perceptions used to assess undergraduate research experience. *The Journal of Higher Education, 74*(2), 210–230.

Beede, D., Julian, T., Langdon, D., McKittrick, G., Khan, B., & Doms, M. (2011). *Women in STEM: A gender gap to innovation*. Washington, DC: U.S. Department of Commerce Economics and Statistics Administration.

Bowman, P. J. (2006). Role strain and adaptation issues in the strength-based model: Diversity, multilevel, and life-span considerations. *Counseling Psychologist, 34*(1), 118–133.

Bowman, P. J. (2013). A strengths-based social psychological approach to resiliency: Cultural diversity, ecological and life span issues. In S. Prince-Embury (Ed.), *Resilience in children, adolescents, and adults* (pp. 299–325). New York, NY: Springer.

Bowman, P. J., & St. John, E. P. (2011). Toward a 21st-century meritocracy: Bridging scholarship, intervention research, and social change. In P. J. Bowman & E. P. St. John (Eds.), *Diversity, merit, and higher education: Readings on equal education* (pp. 325–348). New York, NY: AMS Press.

Brazziel, M. E., & Brazziel, F. B. (2001). Factors in decisions of underrepresented minorities to forego science and engineering doctoral study: A pilot study. *Journal of Science Education and Technology, 10*, 273–281.

Chubin, D. E., DePass, A. L., & Blockus, L. (Eds.). (2010). *Understanding interventions that broaden participation in research careers*. Summary of a Conference in Bethesda, MD, May 7–9, 2009. Bethesda, MD: American Society for Cell Biology.

Committee on Institutional Cooperation. (2008). *Collective impact: 50 years of strategic collaboration*. Retrieved from http://www.cic.net/docs/default-source /news-pub/50thanniversary.pdf

Cook, T. D., & Campbell, D. T. (1979). *Quasi-experimentation: Design and analysis issues for field settings*. Boston, MA: Houghton Mifflin.

DeBerard, M. S., Spielmans, G. I., & Julka, D. C. (2004). Predictors of academic achievement and retention among college freshman: A longitudinal study. *College Student Journal, 38*, 66–80.

Dennis, J. M., Phinney, J. S., & Chuateco, L. I. (2005). The role of motivation, parental support and peer support in the academic success of ethnic minority first-generation college students. *Journal of College Student Development, 46*(3), 223–236.

DePass, A. L., & Chubin, D. E. (Eds.). (2009). *Understanding interventions that encourage minorities to pursue research careers: Building a community of research and practice.* Summary of a Conference in Atlanta, GA, May 2–4, 2008. Bethesda, MD: American Society for Cell Biology.

Donaldson, S. I. (2007). *Program theory-driven evaluation science: Strategies and applications*. Mahwah, NJ: Erlbaum.

Fagen, A. P., & Labov, J. B. (2007). Understanding interventions that encourage minorities to pursue research careers: Major questions and appropriate methods. *CBE Life Science Education, 6*(3), 187–189.

George, Y. S., Neale, D. S., Van Horne, V., & Malcolm, S. M. (2001). *In pursuit of a diverse science, technology, engineering, and mathematics workforce: Recommended research priorities to enhance participation by underrepresented minorities.* Washington, DC: American Association for the Advancement of Science.

Greene, J. P., & Winters, M. A. (2005). *Public high school graduation and college-readiness rates: 1991–2002.* New York, NY: Center for Civic Innovation, Manhattan Institute.

Hill, C., Corbett, C., & St. Rose, A. (2010). *Why so few? Women in science, technology, engineering and mathematics.* Washington, DC: American Association of University Women.

Hoyle, R. H., Harris, M. J., & Judd, C. M. (2002). *Research methods in social relations.* Belmont, CA: Wadsworth.

Hunter, A. B., Laursen, S. L., & Seymour, E. (2006). Becoming a scientist: The role of undergraduate research in students' cognitive, personal, and professional development. *Science Education, 91*, 36–74.

James, S. A. (1994). John Henryism and the health of African-Americans. *Culture Medicine and Psychiatry, 18*, 163–182.

James, S. A., Hartnett, S. A., & Kalsbeek, W. D. (1983). John Henryism and blood pressure differences among Black men. *Journal of Behavioral Medicine, 6*, 259–278.

Lopatto, D. (2004). Survey of undergraduate research experiences (SURE): First findings. *Cell Biology Education, 3*, 270–277.

Lopatto, D. (2007). Undergraduate research experiences support science career decisions and active learning. *CBE-Life Sciences Education, 6*(4), 297–306.

Mark, M. M., Donaldson, S. I., & Campbell, B. (2011). *Social psychology and evaluation*. New York, NY: Gilford.

Mark, M. M., & Henry, G. T. (2004). The mechanisms and outcomes of evaluation influence. *Evaluation, 10*(1), 35–57.

Maton, K. I., Domingo, M. R. S., Stolle-McAllister, K. E., Zimmerman, J. L., & Hrabowski, F. A., III. (2009). Enhancing the number of African-Americans who pursue STEM PhDs: Meyerhoff Scholarship Program outcomes, processes, and individual predictors. *Journal of Women and Minorities in Science and Engineering, 15*(1), 15–37.

Maton, K. I., & Hrabowski, F. A., III. (2004). Increasing the number of African American PhDs in the sciences and engineering: A strengths-based approach. *American Psychologist, 59*(6), 547–556.

Maton, K. I., Hrabowski, F. A., & Schmitt, C. L. (2000). African American college students excelling in the sciences: College and postcollege outcomes in the Meyerhoff Scholars Program. *Journal of Research in Science Teaching, 37*(7), 629–654.

Maton, K. I., Pollard, S. A., McDougall Weise, T. V., & Hrabowski, F. A. (2012). Meyerhoff Scholars Program: A strengths based, institution wide approach to increasing diversity in science, technology, engineering, and mathematics. *Mount Sinai Journal of Medicine: A Journal of Translational and Personalized Medicine, 79*(5), 610–623.

National Action Council for Minorities in Engineering, Inc. (2008). *Confronting the "new" American dilemma—Underrepresented minorities in engineering: A data-based look at diversity*. White Plains, NY: Author.

National Research Council. (2009). *Rising above the gathering storm two years later: Accelerating progress toward a brighter economic future*. Washington, DC: The National Academies Press.

National Science Foundation. (2013). *Women, minorities and persons with disabilities in science and engineering: 2013*. Arlington, VA: Author.

Olson, S., & Fagen, A. P. (2007). *Understanding interventions that encourage minorities to pursue research careers: Summary of a workshop*. Washington, DC: National Academies Press.

Pender, M., Marcotte, D. E., Domingo, M. R. S., & Maton, K. I. (2010). The STEM pipeline: The role of summer research experience in minority students' Ph.D. aspirations. *Education Policy Analysis Archives, 18*(30). Retrieved from http://epaa.asu.edu/ojs/article/view/741/871

Perna, L. W. (2006). Studying college choice: A proposed conceptual model. In J. C. Smart (Ed.), *Higher education: Handbook of theory and research* (Vol. 21, pp. 99–157). Dordrecht, The Netherlands: Springer.

Reyes, E. A. (2002). *Extended family support as a protective factor among college students: An exploratory multi-ethnic study* (Unpublished doctoral dissertation). Northwestern University, Evanston, IL.

Robbins, S. B., Lauver, K., Le, H., Davis, D., Langley, R., & Carlstrom, A. (2004). Do psychosocial and study skill factors predict college outcomes? A meta-analysis. *Psychological Bulletin, 130*(2), 261–288.

Russell, S. H., Hancock, M. P., & McCullough, J. (2006). *Evaluation of NSF support for undergraduate research opportunities: Follow-up survey of undergraduate NSF program participants*. Unpublished manuscript, SRI International, Menlo Park, CA.

Russell, S. H., Hancock, M. P., & McCullough, J. (2007). Benefits of undergraduate research experiences. *Science, 316*(5824), 548–549.

Sedlacek, W. E. (2004). *Beyond the big test: Noncognitive assessment in higher education*. San Francisco, CA: Jossey-Bass.

Shadish, W. R., Cook, T. D., & Campbell, D. T. (2002). *Experimental and quasi-experimental design for generalized causal inference*. New York, NY: Houghton Mifflin.

Shadish, W. R., Cook, T. D., & Leviton, L. C. (1991). *Foundations of program evaluation: Theories of practice*. Newbury Park, CA: Sage.

Stage, F. K. (Ed.). (2007). *New Directions for Institutional Research: No. 133. Answering critical questions using quantitative data.* San Francisco, CA: Jossey-Bass.

St. John, E. P. (2003). *Refinancing the college dream: Access, equal opportunity, and justice for taxpayers.* Baltimore, MD: Johns Hopkins University Press.

St. John, E. P. (2006). *Education and the public interest: School reform, public finance, and access to higher education.* Dordrecht, The Netherlands: Springer.

St. John, E. P., Fisher, A. S., Williams, K. L., & Daun-Barnett, N. (2008). *Educational opportunity in Indiana: A study of the twenty-first century scholars program.* Indianapolis, IN: Lumina Foundation for Education.

St. John, E. P., Hu, S., & Fisher, A. S. (2011). *Breaking through the access barrier: Academic capital formation informing public policy.* New York, NY: Routledge.

St. John, E. P., & Musoba, G. D. (2010). *Pathways to academic success: Expanding opportunity for underrepresented students.* New York, NY: Routledge.

White House. (n.d.). *Educate to innovate.* Retrieved from http://www.whitehouse .gov/issues/education/k-12/educate-innovate

Yauch, C. A. (2007, October). *The impact of undergraduate research experiences on graduate school pursuit by industrial engineers.* Unpublished paper presented at the 37th Annual ASEE/IEE Frontiers in Education Conference, Milwaukee, WI.

Zajacova, A., Lynch, S. M., & Espenshade, T. J. (2005). Self-efficacy, stress, and academic success in college. *Research in Higher Education, 46*(6), 677–706.

KRYSTAL L. WILLIAMS is an American Educational Research Association (AERA) Postdoctoral Fellow in the Center for Academic and Workforce Readiness and Success at Educational Testing Services (ETS).

3

This chapter uses a critical quantitative approach to study models and measures of civic engagement for Latina/o college students. The chapter describes the importance of a critical quantitative approach to study civic engagement of Latina/o college students, then uses Hurtado et al.'s (2012) model to examine the civic engagement of Latina/o college students. Alternative and additional measures of civic engagement are described, such as ethnic and indigenous identity, immigrant generation and status, nativity, and time of arrival in the United States. I conclude with recommendations for future models and research on civic engagement of Latina/o college students.

Civic Engagement Measures for Latina/o College Students

Cynthia M. Alcantar

Although college participation in the United States has steadily increased over the past four decades, two- and four-year college degree attainment among 25–64-year-olds has remained stagnant at approximately 39% (Lumina Foundation for Education, 2013a). The lack of growth in college degree holders has led to a shift in higher education policy priorities to focus on increasing educational attainment. The Obama administration has committed to two goals: (a) to ensure that all Americans have the ability to pursue college, and (b) for the United States to have the highest proportion of young adults (a 50% increase nationwide) with college degrees compared to other developed nations by 2020 (The White House, 2009, 2012).

The college completion agenda has been framed as a national priority mainly driven by an economic rationale—to reduce the unemployment rate, increase state and federal tax revenues, and regain global competitiveness (U.S. Department of Education, Office of the Under Secretary, and Office of Postsecondary Education, 2012). While the alignment between higher education and employment is important, the economic rationale underlying the college completion agenda can be problematic. The college completion agenda does not take into account continuing disparities in educational attainment by race and class. While the educational attainment rate has steadily increased for all students in the aggregate, the gap between White

NEW DIRECTIONS FOR INSTITUTIONAL RESEARCH, no. 158 © 2014 Wiley Periodicals, Inc.
Published online in Wiley Online Library (wileyonlinelibrary.com) • DOI: 10.1002/ir.20043

students and students of color persists. In 1996, 35.1% of Asians, 24.8% of Whites, 16.8% of Blacks, and 11.3% of Latina/os held an associate's or bachelor's degree (National Center for Education Statistics [NCES], 2013). These educational attainment gaps continued to be seen in 2009, 65.6% of Asians, 44.9% of Whites, 24.7% of African Americans, and 17.9% of Latina/os ages 25–29 had attained a college degree (Lumina Foundation for Education, 2013b).[1] The question remains, how can institutions, educators, and policy makers provide equal opportunities for all students to attain a college degree?

Moreover, the heavy focus on employment outcomes overshadows other key functions of higher education. Higher education institutions were initially built upon a mission to serve the community and are positioned to actively promote students' civic engagement (Coley & Sum, 2012). Higher education has been a driving mechanism for serving society by developing students' civic engagement, and training leaders and participants of a diverse democracy (Hurtado, 2007; Lopez & Kiesa, 2009).

Researchers have found a positive relationship between educational outcomes (academic achievement and college attainment) and civic engagement (Astin & Sax, 1998; Coley & Sum, 2012; Hillygus, 2005). The literature demonstrates civic engagement and higher education outcomes are mutually reinforcing. Students who are civically engaged are more academically successful and attain higher levels of education (Astin, Vogelgesang, Ikeda, & Yee, 2000). Educational outcomes measures, such as high school and college academic achievement (e.g., SAT scores and grade point averages), have a positive relationship with civic participation (Hillygus, 2005). Individuals with higher levels of education are in turn more civically engaged (Coley & Sum, 2012; Ramakrishnan & Espenshade, 2001). Civic engagement in college also influences future civic participation and postbaccalaureate outcomes. A longitudinal study by Astin and Sax (1998) found that students who volunteered in college were more likely to enroll in graduate school and were more "committed to … promoting racial understanding" (p. 256). So how can institutions, educators, and policy makers foster civic engagement among all students, specifically students of color?

A critical examination of civic engagement of Latina/o college students is important because it examines its role in attainment for a population that is rapidly growing and has low college completion rates. Latina/os are already the largest ethnic minority population accounting for 14% of the U.S. population; by 2050 they are projected to be 29% of the population (Passel & Cohn, 2008). Because civic engagement and college attainment are mutually reinforcing, and given the significant demographic shifts due to immigration, it is vital to closely examine the civic participation of Latina/os in higher education. Civic engagement can potentially be one of the mechanisms through which this population can increase their degree attainment.

In this chapter, I use a quantitative approach (Stage, 2007) to critically examine models and measures of civic engagement for Latina/o college students. First, I introduce the importance of using a critical approach to study the civic engagement of Latina/o college students. Then, I present a model of student success that could guide the development of a new civic engagement model in higher education. In particular, I define and discuss measures of civic engagement that are typically used in higher education research and then provide a set of alternate measures based on factors that impact civic engagement for Latina/os specifically. Finally, I provide recommendations for future directions for models and research on civic engagement of Latina/o college students.

The Critical Quantitative Approach

Here, I examine theoretical models that have been used in the higher education literature to examine civic engagement of college students and to scrutinize whether those models did or did not fit with Latina/o student's experiences. Traditional models of student engagement and success in college were developed from a traditional student perspective, commonly White, middle class, 18–24-years-old, four-year college students, and males (Bensimon, 2007). Models that help us understand student engagement and success often neglect the experiences of ethnic and racial minority, low-income, and community college students (Bensimon, 2007). Thus, institutional policies and classroom pedagogies and practices that have been developed using those models often fail at meeting the goal to engage students and increase student success with nontraditional students (Bensimon, 2007). This is important given the changing demography of Latina/os in the United States, increasing college enrollments, and low postsecondary attainment rates of Latina/o students. Few researchers have asked critical research questions about civic participation among students of color, or have been critical about the indicators and measures of civic engagement of students, especially for Latina/os. In addition, civic engagement has been measured primarily with an emphasis on political engagement, while ignoring other forms of civic engagement.

In my own personal college experience as a low-income first-generation Latina college student, I had to work more than three jobs at a time to help my parents and myself survive, all while attending college full-time so that I could continue to receive financial aid to pay for school. I worked for a public hospital in a low-income community specifically with undocumented and Spanish monolingual patients and my off-campus work–study job was at a public elementary school teaching reading, writing, and math to recently immigrated students from Mexico and Vietnam. On top of working over 40 hours a week and attending school full-time, I independently tutored and mentored students, and coached track at my high school alma mater which was predominantly Latina/o and low-income

NEW DIRECTIONS FOR INSTITUTIONAL RESEARCH • DOI: 10.1002/ir

students. I did not have an official regular 20-hour week volunteer schedule or site; I was not doing it via a program, class, or internship. My volunteer activities were sporadic, but regular in that I was frequently giving back to my community in a variety of ways. Secondly, in my college the type of community involvement I was doing was not rewarded, praised, or reinforced by college educators. The students in my classes who received positive affirmations were those who were able to participate through clubs, Greek life, and internships.

According to traditional civic and educational engagement models I was not engaged in school or my community. I was unable to volunteer long-term for a set 20 hours a week, as a working commuter student I was unable to engage on-campus, and as a first-generation college student, didn't know how or who to ask. Because of students like me, with the growth of college enrollment from low-income students of color, especially at community colleges, it is critical that researchers use a critical quantitative perspective to analyze and develop conceptual models, programs, and pedagogies that are inclusive and considerate of students' experiences in order to engage students and lead them to be successful college graduates who are civically responsible leaders and engaged citizens.

Conceptual Model for Civic Engagement of Latina/os

The theory of participatory democracy originally created by Pateman in 1970 to understand political participation has been used by some researchers as a conceptual model to examine civic engagement in higher education (Spiezio, 2009). Spiezio (2009) writes, "[Participatory democracy] theory specifies the causal relationships that link institutions, individuals, and democratic practice, while also suggesting practical steps that can be taken to promote engaged citizenship" (p. 88). The theory as used in higher education highlights the importance and responsibility of institutions as sites for teaching and fostering democratic principles with particular focus on the classroom (Spiezio, 2009). However, the theory focuses on the institution and classroom and does not recognize external factors that impact student's civic participation. Spiezio's conceptual model is limited and does not reflect the patterns of participation for diverse students, the impact of educational agents (e.g., faculty, administrators, and staff), external factors related to participation, and educational outcomes of civic engagement.

Existing models of student success in higher education are better at incorporating civic engagement of Latina/o college students. Using Hurtado, Alvarez, Guillermo-Wann, Cuellar, and Arellano's (2012) Multicontextual Model for Diverse Learning Environments (DLE Model), I examined the civic engagement of Latina/o students on college campuses. This multicontextual model takes a holistic approach to analyzing the ecosystem of higher education institutions and student success. At the microsystem and mesosystem levels, the model draws on social identity theory, describing the interactions between diverse students with multiple social identities and instructors, staff, and students. Interactions include in- and out-of-class experiences, both social and academic. Institutions and students are also influenced by the community context and external commitments. This model highlights the impact of macrosystems on institutions and students. This includes sociohistorical and policy contexts that influence institutional contexts. All these systems then influence the climate for diversity and result in greater social equity and success for students of color. The DLE framework represents the reality for Latina/o students and their social and academic engagement at the institutions they attend, impacting their civic engagement, academic success, and degree attainment.

Defining and Measuring Political and Social Civic Engagement

To be civically engaged is to be motivated to take action politically or nonpolitically to make a positive impact within a community (O'Connor, 2006). There are different types and ways to be civically engaged. Most past research has focused on *political* civic engagement, such as voting, but the most current, albeit limited work has included other forms of civic engagement behaviors that are indirectly related to politics, for example, volunteering in the community. Inconsistencies exist in the literature regarding what researchers identify, and the ways that they measure, various forms of *social* civic engagement behaviors (Newell, 2011).

Political Civic Engagement. Studies of *political* civic engagement examine civic and political knowledge, political socialization of children, political attitudes and perceptions, citizenship, and voting behaviors (Coley & Sum, 2012; Hillygus, 2005; McIntosh & Munoz, 2009; Torney-Purta, 2002). The studies on political civic engagement include behaviors directly related to political participation, such as voting, active participation in a political organization or club, protesting, or working as a poll-worker or on a campaign, or a measurement of political knowledge. These studies have mostly focused on White middle-class students in high school and four-year colleges (Hillygus, 2005).

Using these narrow indicators of civic engagement, Latina/os are found to be less civically engaged. Studies using political civic engagement as a sole indicator for civic participation have found Latina/os to be less civically and politically engaged, demonstrate less political knowledge, participate less in elections, and express lower levels of trust in the political system (Coley & Sum, 2012; Ramakrishnan & Espenshade, 2001; Torney-Purta, Barber, & Wilkenfeld, 2007). However, using a critical quantitative perspective demonstrates that research that narrowly conceptualizes civic engagement for Latina/os reinforces a deficit perspective on participation of people of color. A focus on voting activities as a sole measure of civic engagement misses a large segment of ethnic minority and immigrant populations who are not U.S.-born or naturalized citizens, and who are not

Table 3.1. Civic Engagement Variables in BPS:09 Data Set

Political Civic Engagement	Political or Social Civic Engagement	Social Civic Engagement
Registered to vote Ever voted in '04 (2004) Voted in '04 elect. (2006) Ever voted in '09 (2009)	Fundraising Service to nonprofit orgs (2009)	Tutoring, Mentoring Neighborhood improvement, Clean-up Hospital, Nursing Home (2004) Health services (2006, 2009) Homeless shelter, Soup kitchen Service to church Other work with kids

Note: Unless year is specified, variables were available all the years BPS was administered.

allowed to vote in federal elections and some state and local elections (U.S. Citizenship and Immigration Services, 2014). These federal or state political participation laws stand at the macro level of the DLE model taking into account the policy context that impacts engagement (as well as student success) in diverse learning environments. To that I would add civic participation. Although undocumented and resident Latina/os do not vote, they may be politically civically engaged by participating in local community elections, school boards, or rallies. They may also display social civic engagement by participating in community organizing, mentoring, or working civil service jobs (e.g., tutoring), behaviors that are not typically captured in the national data sets that are commonly used to study civic engagement.

One example of measures narrowly focusing on voting as an indicator of *political* civic engagement in is the Beyond Postsecondary Students (BPS:09) national data set. A critical examination of the civic engagement variables in the BPS:09 data set reveals limited, ambiguous, and skewed civic engagement indicators. Table 3.1 presents civic engagement variables in the BPS:09 data set as a continuum of participation with *political* civic engagement at one end and *social* civic engagement at the opposite end. First, political civic engagement measures are focused on voting, the intention and action to vote. This gives the respondent only one way to demonstrate their political civic engagement. Secondly, the data set contains two vague civic engagement answer choices which create ambiguity for the respondent. The middle column of Table 3.1 includes variables that represent either side of the civic engagement continuum. For example, *fundraising* depends on the focus, mission, or goals for raising money. A student fundraising for a political campaign represents political civic engagement, whereas fundraising for their local public school would align with social civic engagement. Lastly, the civic engagement measures in the data set are skewed toward social civic engagement measures.

Social Civic Engagement.   Although Latina/os may be less engaged in formal and traditionally defined political civic activities, there are nontraditional ways to be civically engaged, politically and socially. The extent to which studies examine *social* civic engagement, the concept, has been observed or operationalized in multiple ways. The literature refers to social civic engagement using a variety of terms, including community-based civic engagement, prosocial behaviors, humanitarian/civic involvement, civic activities, expressive activities, and social activities (Newell, 2011; Stepick, Stepick, & Labissiere, 2008). Social civic engagement includes behaviors and activities that directly impact the community and may indirectly impact government, such as volunteering, participating in community-based organizations (CBOs), and tutoring students. However, most research has narrowly focused on volunteering as a social civic engagement measure (McIntosh & Munoz, 2009; Tong, 2010).

Most research on social civic engagement is limited and does not incorporate other nontraditional measures of social civic engagement. For example, Tong (2010) examined rates of volunteerism among immigrant youth as a measure of acculturation using data from the National Longitudinal Study of Adolescent Health. She found that 45% of immigrant adolescents had volunteered ($N = 3,266$). The results revealed that students who were most likely to volunteer were: Asian immigrants (compared to Latina/os), those with higher aspirations to attend college, and those whose parents attained at least a high school diploma (Tong, 2010). She also found that immigrant youth who lived in affluent neighborhoods were more likely to volunteer while those who grew up in underserved communities were more likely to volunteer as adults (Tong, 2010). More affluent immigrant students may have larger social networks, more opportunities to engage in volunteer work, and may also be more engaged with volunteering in preparation for college admissions. Tong's (2010) work aligns with other research that has found that ethnic minority and low-income students have fewer opportunities to learn and practice civic engagement.

The limited scope of social civic engagement behaviors is problematic for Latina/o populations who may be civically engaged, but not in a traditional and normative manner. Some researchers have expressed the importance of expanding the traditional view of civic engagement so that it incorporates social civic engagement behaviors that have been found to engage ethnic minorities and/or immigrant communities, such as translating for the community, tutoring, and mentoring youth (Perez, Cortes, Ramos, & Coronado, 2010; Perez, Espinoza, Ramos, Coronado, & Cortes, 2010; Stepick et al., 2008).

At the center of the DLE model is the relationship of student's social identity (e.g., race, class, and gender, and I would add immigrant identities), and climate for diversity and student success. Latina/o students, especially immigrants, are more likely to be civically engaged in activities that are connected to their ethnic and/or immigrant identities (Perez, Cortes, et al., 2010; Perez, Espinoza, et al., 2010; Stepick et al., 2008); however the activities in which they are likely to engage are not consistently or accurately measured in studies on civic engagement of college students (Hillygus, 2005). Returning to the BPS:09 data set measures, additional social and political civic engagement measures that could be incorporated to be more inclusive and considerate of Latina/o and other ethnic minority populations include service to the community, work with the elderly, community organizing, marching or protesting, and volunteering in a campaign or as a poll-worker.

Social Identity and Sociohistorical and Policy Context. In addition to considering the most appropriate civic engagement measures when studying the civic engagement of Latina/o students, researchers must also critically examine the participant's immigrant background (social identity part of the microsystem level of DLE Model) and the historical context (see, sociohistorical and policy context of DLE Model) during data collection.

Social Identity: Immigrant Generation and Status. Civic engagement is influenced by student's social identity which is shaped by intersections of race, class, gender, and immigrant backgrounds. For Latina/os, many of whom are of immigrant backgrounds, it is important to examine relationships between civic participation and immigrant generation,[2] immigration status (U.S.-born, resident, refugee, undocumented, or the most recent, Deferred Action for Childhood Arrivals—DACA), and length of time in the United States (Tong, 2010; Uslaner & Conley, 2003).

Immigrant generation has an impact on civic engagement, and in particular the type of civic engagement. Recent immigrants are more likely to be socially civically engaged, while second- and first-generation immigrants who have been in the United States for a longer period of time are more likely to demonstrate higher levels of political civic engagement (Uslaner & Conley, 2003). The 1.5-generation immigrant may also differ in their civic engagement and participation from first- and second-generation immigrants. On the one hand, 1.5-generation immigrants share an affinity to the United States since they spent much of their schooling in the United States, but may still face similar issues as first-generation immigrants (Seif, 2011). Higher levels of political participation may be due to their political and cultural socialization in U.S. schools.

To demonstrate the relationship between immigration generation and time in the United States on civic engagement, a study on Chinese immigrants in Los Angeles' Chinatown (Uslaner & Conley, 2003) found that recent immigrants and older adults were less likely to be engaged in American politics compared to their U.S.-born and younger adult counterparts. However, recent and older Chinese immigrants were more likely to be socially civically engaged through Chinese CBOs (Uslaner & Conley, 2003).

U.S.-born Chinese were also likely to engage with ethnic associations as "a way of protesting the authoritarian government in China that discourages democratic participation" (Uslaner & Conley, 2003, p. 346). Although this study focused on Chinese immigrants, similar patterns might be true for Latina/o immigrants. A critical examination of civic engagement models and measures may find that after controlling for variables representing immigrant generation and time in the United States, civic participation may differ for various subgroups of immigrant Latina/os.

Social Identity: Ethnic Identity and Indigenous Backgrounds. Beyond immigrant generation, Latina/os are very diverse. Aside from diverse immigrant experiences, Latina/os are ethnically diverse representing all Latin-American countries, they speak a variety of languages and dialects (e.g., in Mexico alone, aside from the official language of Spanish, there are 62 indigenous languages), practice various religions, come from countries with differing political contexts, and represent various indigenous communities (Seif, 2011). Even within each ethnic group, there may be differences in civic participation among indigenous populations. For example, there are various Mexican indigenous enclaves in the United States, such as Oaxaqueños in southern California. These students are engaged in activities that promote and support their indigenous Mexican identities and communities, such as teaching younger students ballet folklorico (traditional dances) while mentoring them. Latina/os' diverse backgrounds affect their schooling, and college access and attainment, but may also affect civic participation.

Sociohistorical and Policy Context: Historical Context of Civic Engagement Studies. The historical context of a study is important to consider when examining civic engagement, especially for racial and ethnic minority and immigrant populations (McIntosh & Munoz, 2009; Ramakrishnan & Espenshade, 2001; Stepick et al., 2008; Torney-Purta, Amadeo, & Andolina, 2010). Civic participation rates are influenced by current social and political events which are embedded in a historical context, especially when they have the potential to negatively affect particular communities. Researchers have found higher political participation among immigrant communities when anti-immigrant legislation is presented in the ballots (Ramakrishnan & Espenshade, 2001). For example, Banda (2010) found that in 2006 authorized and unauthorized immigrant youth across various metropolitan cities in the United States participated in rallies, walk-outs, marches, and meetings to support undocumented students. Regions that are heavily populated with immigrants, like the Chicago metropolitan area, demonstrate higher rates of civic participation by immigrant populations compared to regions where immigrants are less concentrated or face harsh anti-immigrant policies, such as Arizona (Donnelly, 2010).

Stepick and his colleagues (2008) examined the civic engagement of immigrant youth in Florida and found that some of the higher rates of civic engagement among participants may have been due to the impact of the

Elian case, a Cuban boy who was found drifting to Florida from Cuba on a floating device with his dead mother (Stepick et al., 2008). In a longitudinal study of the civic engagement of high school students, McIntosh and Munoz (2009) found increased levels of political discussion in the classroom and a strong relationship between African-American high school students and their intention to vote. Students were surveyed in 2009, months after President Obama was elected into office. During this time, eligible Black, Hispanic, and Asian voters exhibited higher turnout rates than in 1992 elections (Coley & Sum, 2012). The researchers assume these patterns emerged due to the historical context of the study, when the first Black presidential candidate campaigned for and took office in the United States, which may have inspired more students of color to vote (McIntosh & Munoz, 2009). This coincides with other findings of high voting rates among minorities during the 2008 presidential elections (Coley & Sum, 2012).

New Directions for a Critical Quantitative Approach to Study Civic Engagement

A critical quantitative perspective is the most appropriate approach to (a) critically examine past models and studies of engagement in higher education, and specifically question the inclusive and/or exclusive nature of the models, research questions, and measures; (b) develop more inclusive civic engagement measures, including the expansion of social and political civic engagement indicators to incorporate nontraditional civic engagement activities; and (c) develop a new model of civic engagement in higher education that takes into consideration external factors that impact the civic engagement patterns of students of color, including ethnic and social identity, immigrant generation and status, and sociohistorical and policy contexts.

Overall, more research is needed on the civic engagement of students of color in higher education. Research is particularly needed on high-impact practices that dually promote civic and academic engagement for college students, such as service learning. In general, research on service learning has not captured the experiences of Latina/os and other nontraditional students. This work is vital because higher education institutions are in immediate need of high-impact practices to achieve degree attainment goals. Also, future studies on civic engagement must consider the unique participation of specific ethnic and racial minority students. Possibly, similar inconsistencies in civic participation patterns using traditional measures and models would be found for American Indian, Black, and Asian American and Pacific Islander college students.

Lastly, an updated civic engagement model for higher education must be developed to guide research to better understand civic engagement, the development of civic engagement values and participation, the role of educators and higher education institutions, and the connection to educational outcomes, especially for Latina/o college students. Such a critical civic engagement model must include a variety of factors that are related to participation of Latina/o college students, such as the DLE model of student success. A civic engagement model developed with a critical quantitative perspective would not only guide new research but also promote institution and faculty understanding regarding ways to socially and academically engage Latina/o students. This would foster democratic and civic values and engagement, ultimately impacting student's academic success and educational attainment.

Notes

1. The attainment rate of Asians is deceiving since there is a bimodal distribution on attainment when disaggregated by ethnicity.
2. First-generation immigrants are those who immigrate to the United States older than 12 years old, 1.5-generation immigrants are those who immigrate to the United States at or under the age of 12, and second-generation immigrants are U.S.-born children of at least one foreign-born parent.

References

Astin, A. W., & Sax, L. J. (1998). How undergraduates are affected by service participation. *Journal of College Student Development, 39,* 251–263.

Astin, A. W., Vogelgesang, L. J., Ikeda, E. K., & Yee, J. A. (2000). *How service learning affects students.* Retrieved from http://heri.ucla.edu/PDFs/HSLAS/HSLAS.PDF

Banda, X. (2010). Immigrant youth are emerging actors. In X. Bada, J. Fox, R. Donnelly, & A. Selee (Eds.), *Context matters: Latino immigrant civic engagement in nine U.S. cities.* Washington, DC: Woodrow Wilson International Center for Scholars.

Bensimon, E. M. (2007). Presidential address: The underestimated significance of practitioner knowledge in the scholarship on student success. *The Review of Higher Education, 30,* 441–469.

Coley, R. J., & Sum, A. (2012). *Fault lines in our democracy: Civic knowledge, voting behavior, and civic engagement in the United States.* Princeton, NJ: Educational Testing Service.

Donnelly, R. (2010). Civic engagement and political participation in nine cities. In X. Bada, J. Fox, R. Donnelly, & A. Selee (Eds.), *Context matters: Latino immigrant civic engagement in nine U.S. cities.* Washington, DC: Woodrow Wilson International Center for Scholars.

Hillygus, D. S. (2005). The missing link: Exploring the relationship between higher education and political engagement. *Political Behavior, 27,* 25–47.

Hurtado, S. (2007). Linking diversity with the educational and civic missions of higher education. *The Review of Higher Education, 30,* 185–196.

Hurtado, S., Alvarez, C. L., Guillermo-Wann, C., Cuellar, M., & Arellano, L. (2012). A model for diverse learning environments: The scholarship on creating and assessing conditions for student success. In J. C. Smart & M. B. Paulsen (Eds.), *Higher education handbook of theory and research* (pp. 41–122). New York, NY: Springer.

Lopez, M. H., & Kiesa, A. (2009). What we know about civic engagement among college students. In B. Jacoby & Associates (Eds.), *Civic engagement in higher education: Concepts and practices* (pp. 31–48). San Francisco, CA: Jossey-Bass.

Lumina Foundation for Education. (2013a). *A stronger nation through higher education: Visualizing data to help us achieve a big goal for college attainment.* Retrieved from

http://www.luminafoundation.org/publications/A_stronger_nation_through_higher
_education-2013.pdf

Lumina Foundation for Education. (2013b). *Lumina foundation strategic plan 2013 to 2016*. Retrieved from http://www.luminafoundation.org/advantage/document/goal _2025/2013-Lumina_Strategic_Plan.pdf

McIntosh, H., & Munoz, M. A. (2009). Predicting civic engagement in urban high school students. *Journal of Research in Character Education, 71*, 41–62.

National Center for Education Statistics (NCES). (2013). *Status and trends in the education of racial and ethnic minorities*. Retrieved from http://nces.ed.gov/pubs2010 /2010015/tables/table_27a.asp

Newell, M. A. (2011). *An exploration of civic engagement of community college students and graduates* (Doctoral dissertation). Retrieved from http://www.rpgroup .org/sites/default/files/AN_EXPLORATION_OF_CIVIC_ENGAGEMENT_OF _COMMUNITY_COLLEGE_STUDENTS_AND_GRADUATES.pdf

O'Connor, J. S. (2006). Civic engagement in higher education. *Change, 38*, 52–58.

Passel, J. S., & Cohn, D. (2008). *U.S. population projections: 2005–2050*. Washington, DC: Pew Research Center.

Perez, W., Cortes, R., Ramos, K., & Coronado, H. (2010). "Cursed and blessed": Examining the socioemotional and academic experiences of undocumented Latina and Latino college students. In J. Price (Ed.), *New Directions for Student Services: No. 131. Understanding and supporting undocumented students* (pp. 35–51). Hoboken, NJ: Wiley.

Perez, W., Espinoza, R., Ramos, K., Coronado, H., & Cortes, R. (2010). Civic engagement patterns of undocumented Mexican students. *Journal of Hispanic Higher Education, 9*, 245–265.

Ramakrishnan, S. K., & Espenshade, T. J. (2001). Immigrant incorporation and political participation in the United States. *The International Migration Review, 35*, 870–909.

Seif, H. (2011). "Unapologetic and unafraid": Immigrant youth come out from the shadows. In C. A. Flanagan & B. D. Christens (Eds.), *New Directions for Child and Adolescent Development: No. 134. Youth civic development: Work at the cutting edge* (pp. 59–75). Hoboken, NJ: Wiley.

Spiezio, K. (2009). Engaging general education. In B. Jacoby & Associates (Eds.), *Civic engagement in higher education: Concepts and practices* (pp. 85–98). San Francisco, CA: Jossey-Bass.

Stage, F. K. (2007). Answering critical questions using quantitative data. In F. K. Stage (Ed.), *New Directions for Institutional Research: No. 133. Using quantitative data to answer critical questions* (pp. 5–16). San Francisco, CA: Jossey-Bass.

Stepick, A., Stepick, C. D., & Labissiere, Y. (2008). South Florida's immigrant youth and civic engagement: Major engagement: Minor differences. *Applied Developmental Science, 12*, 57–65.

Tong, Y. (2010). Foreign-born concentration and acculturation to volunteering among immigrant youth. *Social Forces, 89*, 117–144.

Torney-Purta, J. (2002). The school's role in developing civic engagement: A study of adolescents in twenty-eight countries. *Applied Developmental Science, 6*, 203–212.

Torney-Purta, J., Amadeo, J.-A., & Andolina, M. W. (2010). A conceptual framework and multimethod approach for research on political socialization and civic engagement. In L. R. Sherrod, J. Torney-Purta, & C. A. Flanagan (Eds.), *Handbook of research on civic engagement in youth* (pp. 497–523). Hoboken, NJ: Wiley.

Torney-Purta, J., Barber, C. H., & Wilkenfeld, B. (2007). Latino adolescents' civic development in the United States: Research results from the IEA Civic Education Study. *Journal of Youth Adolescence, 36*, 111–125.

U.S. Citizenship and Immigration Services. (2014). *Should I consider U.S. citizenship?* Retrieved from http://www.uscis.gov/citizenship/learners/should-i-consider -us-citizenship

U.S. Department of Education, Office of the Under Secretary, and Office of Postsecondary Education. (2012). *Advancing civic learning and engagement in democracy: A road map and call to action.* Washington, DC. Retrieved from http://www.ed.gov/sites/default/files/road-map-call-to-action.pdf

Uslaner, E. M., & Conley, R. S. (2003). Civic engagement and particularized trust: The ties that bind people to their ethnic communities. *American Politics Research, 31*, 331–360.

The White House. (2009). *Meeting the nation's 2020 goal: State targets for increasing the number and percentage of college graduates with degrees.* Retrieved from http://www.whitehouse.gov/sites/default/files/completion_state_by_state.pdf

The White House. (2012). *Higher education.* Retrieved from http://www.whitehouse.gov/issues/education/higher-education

CYNTHIA M. ALCANTAR is a research associate for the Institute of Immigration, Globalization, and Education at the University of California, Los Angeles.

NEW DIRECTIONS FOR INSTITUTIONAL RESEARCH • DOI: 10.1002/ir

4

This chapter presents various considerations researchers undertook to conduct a quantitative study on low-income students using a national data set. Specifically, it describes how a critical quantitative scholar approaches guiding frameworks, variable operationalization, analytic techniques, and result interpretation. Results inform how policymakers and school administrators can focus their efforts to improve the academic preparation and college enrollment of low-income students.

Using Large Data Sets to Study College Education Trajectories

Leticia Oseguera, Jihee Hwang

A college education has been and remains a valuable commodity, beneficial to individuals and the broader community (Swail, 2000). An educated individual is more likely to be committed to society, contribute to the economy, and be more financially independent (Perna, 2006; Swail, 2000). However, research by prominent higher education scholars suggests that there are significant disparities in educational pathways after high school among students from different socioeconomic groups (McDonough & Antonio, 1996; Perez & McDonough, 2008; Perna, 2006; Walpole, 2007). Many students do not enroll in higher education, and these students are disproportionately from low-income backgrounds (Horn & Berger, 2005; Orfield, Marin, & Horn, 2005; Rosenbaum, 2001).

As the population of low socioeconomic status (SES) students in the United States continues to expand (Goldrick-Rab & Roksa, 2008; Walpole, 2007), it is essential that educational leaders and policymakers gain a better understanding of the impact their decisions have on individuals' ability to attend college and what types of institutions they attend. This chapter presents the steps we took to examine low-income students and their post-high school transitions. Specifically, we reflect on our design and research questions within a critical quantitative approach and offer readers examples

Portions of this chapter are adapted from the PATHWAYS to Postsecondary Success project supported from Bill & Melinda Gates Foundation. For a full version of the report, refer to Oseguera (2012).

NEW DIRECTIONS FOR INSTITUTIONAL RESEARCH, no. 158 © 2014 Wiley Periodicals, Inc.
Published online in Wiley Online Library (wileyonlinelibrary.com) • DOI: 10.1002/ir.20044

of ways to engage in quantitative work employing asset-based perspectives. We present a narrative of the process and explain how our critical quantitative research design informed our work.

Using the Education Longitudinal Study (ELS), we illustrate how secondary data sets can be used by critical quantitative researchers to compare the post-high school educational trajectories of low-income students to middle-/high-income peers by testing a conceptual framework to better understand if certain factors are more predictive of college enrollment for low-income students compared to their higher income counterparts. The study is guided by two overarching research questions:

1. What are the postsecondary education enrollment trajectories of low-income students and how do these trajectories differ from those of students from middle or higher income backgrounds?
2. Using ELS, how can Oakes's (2003) critical conditions framework contribute to explaining low-income student college enrollment?

Educational Pathways and Critical Conditions

Studies on educational pathways frequently focus on four-year colleges emphasizing baccalaureate degree attainment (Strayer, 2002). Understanding of access to and experiences in the community college and for-profit sector is limited despite the fact that significant proportions of the U.S. population begin postsecondary education (PSE) at community colleges (Cohen & Brawer, 2008) and for-profit college enrollment has increased by 300% from 2000 to 2010 (Aud et al., 2011), with sizable percentages hailing from low-income backgrounds (Tierney & Hentschke, 2007). While baccalaureate degree attainment is laudable, the importance of associate's degrees and certificate attainment for low-income students is also critical especially in light of calls to credential more Americans. Given the fact that community colleges and for-profit schools have a high percentage of low-income students (Chung, 2008; Staklis, Bersudskaya, & Horn, 2011),[1] an expanded understanding of college access necessarily needs to include these institutional types for a full range of available pathways.

Critical Inquiry: Using Relevant Theory.   Jeannie Oakes (2003) proposed seven critical high school conditions aimed to inform policy to reduce disparities that exist in college access among students exposed to different high school environments. Oakes's framework provides a useful lens to examine our research questions as its focus is on school contexts that enable college access and is based on work in educationally and economically disadvantaged communities and schools. The seven conditions are: (a) safe and adequate school facilities (SAF), (b) rigorous academic curriculum (RAC), (c) qualified teachers (QT), (d) a college-going school culture (CGC), (e) intensive academic and social supports (IASS), (f) family–neighborhood–school connections (FNSC), and (g) opportunities

NEW DIRECTIONS FOR INSTITUTIONAL RESEARCH • DOI: 10.1002/ir

to develop a multicultural college-going identity (MCGI). Oakes (2003) noted that students from middle/upper-middle class families enroll in high school environments that satisfy these conditions whereas socioeconomically disadvantaged students might not, but that if these conditions can be created, college enrollment would be more probable an outcome.

Using Oakes's (2003) framework, we investigate the relationship between these conditions and college enrollment separately among low-income students and their middle-/high-income peers. As critical quantitative researchers, it is important to select conceptual guides that are asset based and also examine whether theoretical models explain the phenomena advanced, that is, college access. Although elements of these seven conditions are well supported by literature as encouraging college access, they have yet to be operationalized using a nationally representative database. This step would allow us to further untangle which school-level variables expand college access for low-income students, a population that continues to be understudied. Adapting Oakes's (2003) framework illustrates how critical quantitative researchers advance knowledge via testing, verifying, and modifying theories.

Method

In this section, we describe the data set and some of the ways a critical quantitative researcher can approach the sample and make sample selections. We offer commentary on the benefits and tradeoffs of using large data sets and what to consider when defining terms and selecting analytic procedures.

Data Source and Sample.   The data were drawn from the Education Longitudinal Study (ELS) 2002–2006 panel, collected for the National Center for Education Statistics (NCES). The NCES surveyed 14,000 United States 10th graders in spring 2002, and the respondents were surveyed again in spring 2004 (when students were asked to report their intended high school graduation status) and spring 2006 (two years post-high school, assuming an on-time traditional high school graduation). The final sample of respondents who completed all three surveys included 12,550 youth attending public, religious, and private high schools throughout the United States. To maintain fidelity to the framework, we necessarily needed a data set that contained both individual- and school-level measures. Another strength of the ELS data set for operationalizing our framework was that information was collected from the students, the students' parents, teachers, and school administrators. Oakes (2003) emphasized the role of multiple actors (i.e., student, parent, and teachers) to build a positive school environment. Therefore, including information from multiple perspectives aligns well with the guiding theoretical framework and strengthens the analysis.

Sample size consideration was important for this work given already low population numbers for some of the groups of interest in this study.

NEW DIRECTIONS FOR INSTITUTIONAL RESEARCH • DOI: 10.1002/ir

To avoid sample loss due to missing values that are common problems in survey data analysis, we employed multiple imputation (Rubin, 1987) that uses information from the sample distributions of the variables to replace missing values with randomly generated but contextually appropriate values. The multiple imputation method enabled us to preserve sample size. If we deleted items that had missing values or employed other methods to deal with missing values (e.g., listwise deletion), we could have disproportionately lost cases in the low-income sample, producing a less accurate estimation of the relationship between these conditions and low-income students.

Variables. In this section, we provide the rationale for sample selection (i.e., defining low-income students), the dependent variable (i.e., educational trajectories), and selected independent variables (i.e., Oakes's critical conditions).

Income Measure. There is no consensus on how to define low income. Some scholars argue that income and family size alone do not capture all students who are low income. Scholars suggest measures such as whether a family has trouble paying bills, or whether a family has health benefits are better reflections of income level. Other studies use a threshold of certain dollar amount (see Engle & Tinto, 2008; Paulsen & St. John, 2002) or define income using relative position (e.g., the lowest quartile of the sample; Cabrera & La Nasa, 2000). By applying different measures in diverse contexts, we can obtain a more detailed understanding to improve educational research and practice. At the same time, it is important to acknowledge the tradeoffs one makes in determining the population. For this work, we intentionally modeled the federal designation of poverty level to define low income. Our decision was based on the fact that we want to produce findings that have implications for schools. Schools use these designations for eligibility for certain social services, therefore we also chose to test these models using measures relevant to school definitions. The final unweighted sample size resulted in 4,300 students identified as low income and 8,250 students identified as middle or high income using income adjusted figures to account for family size.[2]

Educational Trajectories. Students' educational pathways were generated using a variety of variables from the ELS. Because the data were longitudinal, we could identify precisely which path each student pursued. In contrast to many other studies on this topic (e.g., the Current Population Survey), the educational attainment figures in the current study were not cross-sectional or based solely on population estimates.

For the first layer, we examined the students' educational pathways two years after their 10th grade year, in 2004. Students were categorized into one of four paths: (a) dropped out of high school; (b) still enrolled in high school; (c) expected to graduate from high school with a diploma or equivalent and had not completed an academic concentrator requirement; or (d) expected to graduate from high school with a diploma or equivalent and had completed an academic concentrator requirement (i.e., were "college ready"). To the extent possible, NCES confirmed the 12th grade status reported by students in this survey.

We traced students' post-high school transitions, two years later in 2006, into college (various types) or elsewhere (e.g., into the military or the labor force). Note that students were classified into nonoverlapping categories. For example, they were considered to have enrolled in PSE if they had entered college (either part-time or full-time), regardless of employment status. We considered the types of colleges they enrolled in: (a) two-year (or less) public or private community college; (b) two-year (or less) proprietary college; (c) four-year proprietary college; or (d) four-year public or private college or university. We then examined whether students de-enrolled or stopped out of college in the two years after completing the 12th grade.

Among the students who did not enter college, we evaluated how many were employed for at least nine months out of a given year (classified as employed in our study); were unemployed for three or more months in a given year (classified as unemployed); or had entered the military. Again, although the experiences of students in this group were diverse (making it difficult to assign a succinct label), for the sake of interpretability this point in time will be referred to as two years post-high school. These classifications demonstrate that complex pathways can be captured in quantitative work. Often, quantitative researchers collapse categories for ease of presentation. While collapsing is unavoidable at times due to limited sample size or other considerations, our work advocates for greater detail to better understand nuances in post-high school pathways depending on the type of graduation status one attains. As Stage (2007) points out, this level of detail enables us to investigate different pathways by high school completion status and improves understandings of those who have been underrepresented (i.e., students who dropped out of high school or who take longer than the typical four years to complete high school) in critical quantitative inquiry.

Associated Variables With Oakes's Critical Conditions. We examine three conditions in our analysis to demonstrate how Oakes's critical conditions contribute to postsecondary enrollment for lower-income students. We selected these three as examples because they each present their own set of advantages and challenges in operationalization. For example, the importance of academic achievement is well documented in the existing literature and is perhaps the most fundamental condition for successful transition from high school to college. That is, students with higher academic achievement or who take advanced coursework are more likely to go to college than their lower achieving counterparts (Lee, 2012; Stearns, Potochnick, Moller, & Southworth, 2010). Thus, RAC variables in this study included items, such as a student's academic coursework GPA, advanced placement coursework, and curricular track (academic or vocational). Although individual-level academic preparation existed, in order to properly define the curriculum we needed school-level measures of curricular rigor. Therefore, not only was it important to determine if the student themselves engaged in this behavior but it was also equally important to measure the availability of a RAC at each school. Given that Oakes's critical conditions are predicated on school-level environments and characteristics of schools to influence a student's college-going behavior, we aggregate each variable from individual respondents by high school to reflect high school conditions in our analysis.

The influence of SAF is well supported by literature in that school violence lowers students' academic achievement (Milam, Furr-Holden, & Leaf, 2010) and low-income students are more likely to be exposed to crowded classrooms which leads to increased school violence (Astor, Meyer, & Behre, 1999). Important for this design was how the students, parents, and counselors might interpret school environments. Therefore, we include variables that indicate students', parents', and counselors' experiences with and attitudes toward safe school climate and selected elements of the physical environment of their high schools.

When addressing MCGI, Oakes (2003) argued that both race and culture are closely related to college-going identity, especially for historically underrepresented students in higher education. Hence, college-going identity should be nurtured to make "students see college-going as integral to their identities" (p. 7). To operationalize the definition of MCGI, we initially included variables such as students' evaluations of whether or not they get along with different racial/ethnic groups, to what extent students value working to help others, and the percentage of full-time teachers from each racial/ethnic group. Although we selected these variables because they potentially reflect environments that foster diversity and help expose students to same racial/ethnic group success, they imperfectly capture what Oakes suggested. As Harper (2011) reminds us, capturing students' complex identities is hard to achieve relying on one measure such as the categorical responses available on the ELS survey. Rather than proceed with caveats that these measures are imperfect or are approximations, it was more appropriate to disclose that this condition simply could not be operationalized with the existing survey items. We revisit this decision later when we discuss challenges with using a survey that was not designed with our guiding framework in mind.

Analyses.   We conducted a two-phased analysis. To answer the first research question, which was to evaluate significant differences in educational pathways by income level, chi-square tests were employed. A chi-square test allows us to determine whether two groups (i.e., low income and higher income) differ in the distribution of educational pathway categories. That is, we can understand the proportional differences of low-income students' college-going and subsequent pathways relative to their middle/higher income counterparts. Additionally, using the odds ratio formula as demonstrated by Agresti (1990) and Rudas (1998), we calculated odds ratios based on the contingency tables of these categorical variables to obtain a sense of the magnitude of the differences in likelihood of obtaining particular educational pathways between low-income and middle-/high-income students.

For the second research question, we used logistic regression analysis to evaluate the relationship between Oakes's critical conditions and low-income students' access to college. Logistic regression is a special form of regression that enables us to test relationships between predictors and a dichotomous-dependent variable (Long & Freese, 2006). In this study, the dependent variable was defined as whether or not a low-income student was enrolled in college by 2004, two years after high school.

This two-phased methodology allowed us to navigate how low-income students differ from middle/higher income students and to test the conceptual framework's contribution to explaining the possible differences. Rather than analyzing whether low-income students were more or less likely to go to college than their higher income counterparts, the advantage of these methods is that it helps identify the areas that researchers or policy makers need to pay attention to enhance low-income students' supportive school environments.

Findings

The findings section is divided into two sections. We first highlight the educational pathways that were produced and then we follow with excerpts from the analyses on the three selected critical conditions.

Low-Income Students' Educational Pathways.   The educational pathway figures that follow can be understood as representative of 100 students. In other words, in most cases numbers (rather than percentages) are used to demonstrate how many out of 100 students took each given path. This method has been used effectively in other reports of educational movement for various populations (see Rivas, Pérez, Álvarez, & Sólorzano, 2007; Sólorzano, Villalpando, & Oseguera, 2005). It is especially useful because it allows the reader to think very concretely and vividly about the distribution of students across possible outcomes.

Figure 4.1 presents educational pathways data only for students 185% or below the poverty line (i.e., low income). When compared to middle-/high-income counterparts (see Figure 4.2), low-income students were 3.77 times more likely to drop out of school before securing high school credentials. Moreover, the college readiness of low-income students was half that of their middle-/high-income counterparts (14 versus 32 out of 100 students). The second layer, which indicates college entrance status two years after high school, also shows significant differences. Regardless of college readiness, many low-income students had not entered PSE within two years of high school exit. Twenty out of 100 middle-/high-income

Figure 4.1. Educational Pathways of Low-Income Students ($N = 1{,}128{,}699$)

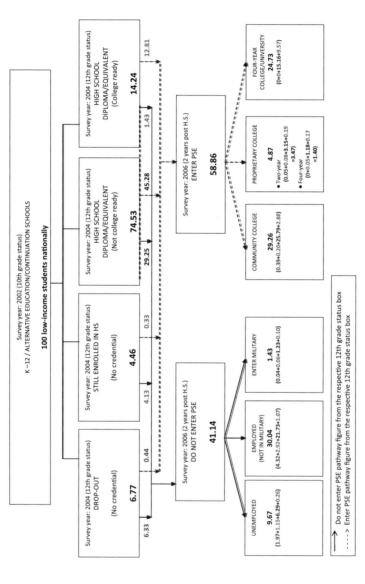

Note: The color-coded numbers allow the reader to trace students' pathways from each 12th grade status. Red numbers (listed first) correspond to students who dropped out of high school, green numbers (listed second) correspond to students who were still enrolled in high school, blue numbers (listed third) correspond to students who graduated from high school not college ready, and pink numbers (listed fourth) correspond to students who did graduate from high school college ready. The numbers within the parenthesis sum to the number immediately above.

Figure 4.2. Educational Pathways of Middle-/High-Income Students ($N = 1,957,955$)

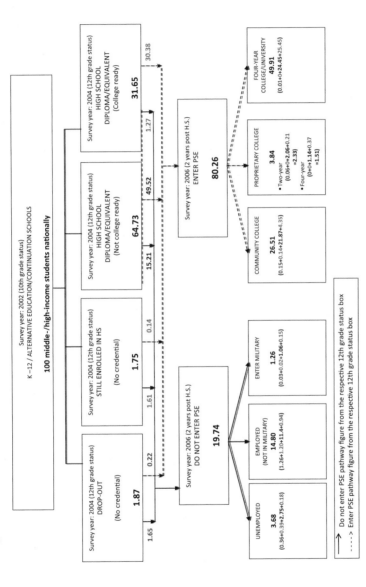

Note: The color-coded numbers allow the reader to trace students' pathways from each 12th grade status. Red numbers (listed first) correspond to students who dropped out of high school, green numbers (listed second) correspond to students who were still enrolled in high school, blue numbers (listed third) correspond to students who graduated from high school not college ready, and pink numbers (listed fourth) correspond to students who did graduate from high school college ready. The numbers within the parenthesis sum to the number immediately above.

students had not entered PSE; however, this figure was more than double (41) for low-income students. Thus, low-income students were 2.84 times more likely not to enter PSE within two years of high school exit.

In addition to whether a student went to college or not, the third layer describes the types of places a student was at two years after high school. Among 41 low-income students who did not enter college, 10 were unemployed, 30 reported employment, and 1 had entered the military. Of the 59 who did enter PSE, 25 students entered four-year colleges, while a greater number (34 students) entered either a community college (29 students) or proprietary college (5 students). Low-income students were 1.27, 2.00, and 2.09 times more likely to begin at four-year for-profit, two-year for-profit, or two-year community colleges, respectively. Middle-/high-income students were 2.27 times more likely to begin PSE at traditional four-year schools. The frequency with which lower income students entered community and proprietary colleges has important implications, as students who do so are less likely to secure credentials beyond a two-year degree if they even secure credentials at all. In fact, one third of low-income students who entered either community colleges (33.2%) or two- or four-year proprietary colleges (30.8% and 33.6%, respectively) had already stopped out within the first two years of entry. This figure was only 14% for students who began at traditional four-year colleges.

Logistic Regression Analysis Results.   Our logistic regression analysis demonstrates how we developed an analytic model based on the second layer of Figure 4.1: college versus no college entrance. This section presents selected findings from the RAC and SAF models. The strongest RAC predictor for college-going among low-income students is whether a student completed an academic concentrator curriculum. A low-income student's odds of attending college increase by 267% if s/he completes a rigorous college preparation curriculum. The next strongest factor that predicts college enrollment is a school context measure, specifically an aggregated teacher's perception that students at the school work hard. That is, for low-income students who attend a school where the teachers report that students work hard, the odds of attending college increase by 197%. Higher individual grade point average also increases the odds of attending college among low-income students.

In comparing the coefficients across the low- and middle-/high-income samples, we see marginally significant differences in the effect across the populations. That is, completing an academic concentrator curriculum and attending a school with a higher mean teacher report that the student body works hard has a stronger positive relationship with college-going among the low-income students, whereas grade point average has a stronger effect among the middle-/high-income students. An interesting finding appears with another school context measure, peer effect. That is, for low-income students, while completing an academic concentrator curriculum has individual benefits for college attendance, attending a school with a larger proportion of students who complete an academic concentrator curriculum actually reduces a low-income student's odds of attending college by 23%. This negative relationship does not surface for the middle-/high-income sample and in fact is one of the stronger positive predictors of college enrollment among the middle-/high-income sample (odds increase by 105%). This finding may reflect the unequal opportunities that low-income students experience even if attending better resourced schools.

Within the SAF variables block, the strongest predictor of college-going for both the low- and middle-/high-income samples is a school context variable measuring a mean parent's opinion of school safety. Attending a school where the parents collectively report that school is safe increases the odds of attending college by 42% for low-income students and 415% for higher income students. While school safety has a positive relationship with college-going for both low-income and middle-income students, it appears that the strength of the relationship is stronger for middle-/high-income students.

Discussion and Conclusion

In conclusion, we summarize the main contributions of this work and propose concepts that critical quantitative researchers should consider when they approach their own work. First, we provide nuanced high school completion figures. That is, we place students into various statuses at the end of a four-year time period, such as stopped out of high school or graduated high school college ready. We move beyond whether or not a student pursues college after high school to investigate more deeply those who do not go on to college, and what they do if they do not enroll in college. The use of nationally representative data helps us clearly demonstrate existing inequality in college access across income levels, which can be informative for future study and developing effective policy. This further warrants the need to examine supportive high school context for low-income students.

Second, we expand college choice options to include the for-profit sector as one type among many that a student pursues after high school completion. The for-profit sector is especially pertinent for low-income students as low-income students are more likely to begin their PSE career in this sector (Chung, 2008; Ruch, 2001). Third, we operate from an asset perspective by adopting a framework that includes positive secondary school conditions that are necessary for student success. Based on logistic regression analysis results, we identified school-level measures that highlight the relationship between school environments and college-going among low-income students and their middle-/high-income peers. We evaluated variables significant to one group but not another and we also identified where certain items operated more strongly for one group over another. This work highlights the importance of considering and addressing the particular needs of low-income students and provides proactive ways for schools to modify their physical and psychological learning environments.

Still, we recommend caution when interpreting the results in this study. Using secondary data sets sometimes makes it difficult to fully operationalize particular constructs. Although we established sufficient evidence of the appropriateness of ELS to operationalize elements in Oakes's critical conditions, as we see in measuring the MCGI subset, survey data limits the capacity to imply individual's internalized value or identity. We must continue our efforts to improve the measurement of such constructs to advance the research and practice. We also need to pay attention to sample loss and complexity. Longitudinal data sets like ELS have specific time points when data are collected from participants and this can create problems. For example, although educational trajectories in our study reflect a point in time close to high school graduation, it also includes the experiences of students who repeated lower grades or who had dropped out and were therefore not in the 12th grade. For the sake of clarity and brevity, this study assumed the various statuses of students in 2004 as the students' 12th grade status. We describe this data set as nationally representative but also recognize that it is likely underreporting special populations or populations difficult to identify such as low-income students who left high school before 10th grade, undocumented students, or students with disabilities.

Finally, we must highlight broader conceptual issues that rarely enter the conversation. We stated initially that college credentials are necessary for economic success, but what does it mean to have a credential with value in the labor market? Who decides? What are the implications of pushing college for all? What are the implications of pushing less than four-year degrees onto low-income students? How should researchers define low income? Critical quantitative researchers seek to investigate the richness of relationships that can be tackled with quantitative data sets and also avoid deficits in examining underserved populations.

The preceding example demonstrates the process that a critical quantitative approach can take when untangling the educational trajectories of low-income youth. Our inquiry was to provide a comprehensive range of post-high school pathways of low-income students, compare how their pathways differ from middle- and high-income peers, and evaluate Oakes's (2003) framework in relation to its contribution to low-income student college access. We hope our reflection on our experience in this particular study will assist institutional researchers interested in employing critical quantitative lenses in their work, and specifically those using large data sets for secondary analysis.

Notes

1. During the 2007–2008 academic year, 51% of for-profit college students and 31% of community college students came from the lowest income quartile, whereas 20% of students in nonprofit four-year colleges did (Staklis et al., 2011).
2. Sample sizes are rounded following the requirement of using restricted-use data sets (see http://nces.ed.gov/statprog/instruct_access_faq.asp).

References

Agresti, A. (1990). *Categorical data analysis*. New York, NY: Wiley.

Astor, R., Meyer, H., & Behre, W. (1999). Unowned places and times: Maps and interviews about violence in high schools. *American Educational Research Journal, 36*(1), 3–42.

Aud, S., Hussar, W., Kena, G., Bianco, K., Frohlich, L., Kemp, J., & Tahan, K. (2011). *The condition of education 2011* (NCES 2011-033). U.S. Department of Education, National Center for Education Statistics. Washington, DC: U.S. Government Printing Office.

Cabrera, A. F., & La Nasa, S. M. (2000). Overcoming the tasks on the path to college for America's disadvantaged. In A. F. Cabrera & S. M. La Nasa (Eds.), *New Directions for Institutional Research: No. 107. Understanding the college choice of disadvantaged students* (pp. 31–43). San Francisco, CA: Jossey-Bass.

Chung, A. (2008). *For-profit student heterogeneity* [MPRA Paper]. Ann Arbor: University of Michigan.

Cohen, A. M., & Brawer, F. B. (2008). *The American community college* (5th ed.). San Francisco, CA: Jossey-Bass.

Engle, J., & Tinto, V. (2008). *Moving beyond access: College success for low-income, first-generation students*. Washington, DC: The Pell Institute for the Study of Opportunity in Higher Education.

Goldrick-Rab, S., & Roksa, J. (2008). *A federal agenda for promoting student success and degree completion*. Washington, DC: Center for American Progress.

Harper, C. E. (2011). Identity, intersectionality, and mixed-methods approaches. In K. A. Griffin & S. D. Museus (Eds.), *New Directions for Institutional Research: No. 151. Using mixed-methods approaches to study intersectionality in higher education* (pp. 103–115). San Francisco, CA: Jossey-Bass.

Horn, L., & Berger, R. (2005). *College persistence on the rise? Changes in 5-year degree completion and postsecondary persistence rates between 1994 and 2000*. Washington, DC: National Center for Education Statistics.

Lee, J. (2012). College for all: Gaps between desirable and actual P-12 math achievement trajectories for college readiness. *Educational Researcher, 42*(2), 43–55.

Long, J. S., & Freese, J. (2006). *Regression models for categorical dependent variables using stata*. College Station, TX: Stata Press.

McDonough, P., & Antonio, A. L. (1996, April). *Ethnic and racial differences in selectivity of college choice*. Paper presented at the annual meeting of the American Educational Research Association, New York, NY.

Milam, A. J., Furr-Holden, C., & Leaf, P. J. (2010). Perceived school and neighborhood safety, neighborhood violence and academic achievement in urban school children. *Urban Review: Issues and Ideas in Public Education, 42*(5), 458–473.

Oakes, J. (2003). *Critical conditions for equity and diversity in college access: Informing policy and monitoring results*. Los Angeles: University of California, UC/ACCORD.

Orfield, G., Marin, P., & Horn, C. L. (2005). *Higher education and the color line: College access, racial equity, and social change*. Cambridge, MA: Harvard Education Press.

Oseguera, L. (2012). *Postsecondary educational pathways of low- and middle/high-income youth: Using the Education Longitudinal Study (ELS) to examine tenth graders' transition from high school*. Los Angeles, CA: UC/ACCORD.

New Directions for Institutional Research • DOI: 10.1002/ir

Paulsen, M. B., & St. John, E. P. (2002). Social class and college costs: Examining the financial nexus between college choice and persistence. *The Journal of Higher Education*, 73(2), 189–236.

Perez, P., & McDonough, P. (2008). Understanding Latina and Latino college choice: A social capital chain migration analysis. *Journal of Hispanic Higher Education*, 7, 249–265.

Perna, L. W. (2006). Studying college access and choice: A proposed conceptual model. In J. C. Smart (Ed.), *Higher education: Handbook of theory and research* (Vol. 21, pp. 99–157). Dordrecht, The Netherlands: Springer.

Rivas, M. A., Pérez, J., Álvarez, C. R., & Sólorzano, D. G. (2007). *An examination of Latina/o transfer students in California's postsecondary institutions* (UCLA Chicano Studies Research Center Report No. 16). Los Angeles, CA: UCLA Chicano Studies Research Center.

Rosenbaum, J. E. (2001). *Beyond college for all: Career paths of the forgotten half.* New York, NY: Russell Sage Foundation.

Rubin, D. B. (1987). *Multiple imputation for nonresponse in surveys.* New York, NY: Wiley.

Ruch, R. S. (2001). *Higher Ed, Inc: The rise of the for-profit university.* Baltimore, MD: The Johns Hopkins University Press.

Rudas, T. (1998). *Odds ratios in the analyses of contingency tables.* Thousand Oaks, CA: Sage Publications.

Sólorzano, D. G., Villalpando, O., & Oseguera, L. (2005). Educational inequities and Latina/o undergraduate students in the United States. *Journal of Hispanic Higher Education*, 4(3), 272–294.

Stage, F. K. (2007). Answering critical questions using quantitative data. In F. Stage (Ed.), *New Directions for Institutional Research: No. 133. Using quantitative data to answer critical question* (pp. 5–16). San Francisco, CA: Jossey-Bass.

Staklis, S., Bersudskaya, V., & Horn, L. (2011). *Students attending for-profit postsecondary institutions: Demographics, enrollment characteristics, and 6-year outcomes* (NCES 2012-173). Washington, DC: U.S. Department of Education. Retrieved from http://nces.ed.gov/pubsearch/pubsinfo.asp?pubid=2012173

Stearns, E., Potochnick, S., Moller, S., & Southworth, S. (2010). High school course-taking and postsecondary institutional selectivity. *Research in Higher Education*, 51, 366–395.

Strayer, W. (2002). The returns to school quality: College choice and earnings. *Journal of Labor Economics*, 20(3), 475–503.

Swail, W. S. (2000). Preparing America's disadvantaged for college: Programs that increase college opportunity. In A. F. Cabrera & S. M. La Nasa (Eds.), *New Directions for Institutional Research: No. 107. Understanding the college choice of disadvantaged students* (pp. 85–101). San Francisco, CA: Jossey-Bass.

Tierney, W. G., & Hentschke, G. C. (2007). *New players, different game: Understanding the rise of for-profit colleges and universities.* Baltimore, MD: The Johns Hopkins University Press.

Walpole, M. B. (2007). *Economically and educationally challenged students in higher education: Access to outcomes* [ASHE Higher Education Report, 33(3)]. San Francisco, CA: Jossey-Bass.

LETICIA OSEGUERA *is associate professor of higher education and senior research associate in the Center for the Study of Higher Education at the Pennsylvania State University.*

JIHEE HWANG *is a PhD candidate and graduate research assistant in the Center for the Study of Higher Education at the Pennsylvania State University.*

5

The author discusses the importance of critical quantitative research for studies of immigrant students, a large and growing group, whose higher education experience is crucial to the future of the United States. The author outlines some of the distinctions to be made among immigrant students and recommends areas of future inquiry.

Critical Quantitative Study of Immigrant Students

Katherine M. Conway

Throughout its history, the United States has attracted large numbers of immigrants. In 2010, the U.S. Census Bureau reported that almost 13% of the U.S. population or 40 million people were foreign-born, four times the number of immigrants in the United States in 1970. Children of immigrants constitute a quarter of all U.S. children (Baum & Flores, 2011). Immigration will be the primary driver of U.S. population growth in the next half century, in part due to the aging baby-boomer population and declining fertility rates, with the result that immigrants are expected to comprise 68 million or 16% of the nation's 420 million residents in 2060 (Armstrong & Ortman, 2013). In the latter half of the 21st century, the United States will be a plurality, with no one group in the majority. Given the size and projected growth of the immigrant population, ongoing critical appraisals of this group's needs, and specifically the different needs of immigrant subgroups, are necessary in order to best direct limited educational resources.

Taking a Critical Quantitative Approach to Studies of Immigrant Students

In addition to the issue of examining the burgeoning immigrant student population, there is the additional issue of effectively addressing the race and/or ethnicity of the immigrant student. Much existing research on students in higher education examines students of different racial/ethnic backgrounds (Perna, 2000; Perna, Li, Walsh, & Raible, 2010; Perna & Titus, 2005; Rendon, Jalomo, & Nora, 2000; Teranishi, 2002). Race/ethnicity, however, is a broad classification that often does injustice to the student groups being studied. Using a pan-ethnic classification such as Asian or Hispanic doesn't sufficiently answer questions about specific groups (Teranishi, 2002). Immigrant students may have concerns that coincide with or supersede those of the broader race/ethnic group of which they are a part, or they may have issues which transcend race/ethnicity and are more comparable to issues faced by native students with similar backgrounds (education, gender, etc.). Thus, the study of immigrant students is burdened by attempts to identify their immigrant status but also to consider other demographic characteristics which may have an impact.

Unfortunately, data on immigrant students are not comprehensive. An important source of data on U.S. undergraduates is the National Postsecondary Student Aid Study (NPSAS:08), a nationally representative sample of more than 100,000 students enrolled in U.S. postsecondary institutions. NPSAS, however, does not collect data on country or region of origin for non-Hispanic immigrant groups and even when country of origin is identified (for Hispanic countries) small sample sizes prevent further analysis. Nor does NPSAS collect information on immigrant arrival in the United States or the type or level of parental education completed in another country. Additionally, NPSAS does not collect information on legal residency status and consequently can provide no information on the approximately 11 million undocumented adult (18 years or older) immigrants, of whom 81% are estimated to have no more than a high school diploma (Camarota & Zeigler, 2009; Staklis, Horn, & Soldner, 2012).

The National Center for Education Statistics (NCES; Staklis et al., 2012) defines immigrant students as foreign-born students who are U.S. citizens with one or both parent(s) born outside the United States, permanent residents, or eligible noncitizens (i.e., those admitted into the United States as legal immigrants for the purpose of obtaining permanent resident alien status). Students born in the United States with at least one foreign-born parent (i.e., children of immigrants) are classified as second generation. If both their parents were born in the United States, students are considered third generation or higher regardless of where they were born. Census Bureau data make the broader distinction between the foreign-born (the individual born outside the United States and its territories) and the native born.

College enrollment and success varies among immigrants as well as their children, and is a function of both country of origin and age at immigration (Baum & Flores, 2011; Erisman & Looney, 2007; Patten, 2012). Conway's (2009, 2010) research classifies students into slightly different groups: native students; native students with immigrant parents; U.S. high schooled immigrant students (born outside of the United States who immigrated early enough to complete high school in the United States) and foreign high schooled immigrant students (who attended high school abroad or received a General Equivalency Diploma). Education literature often uses the term generation 1.5 to distinguish those who immigrate as children from the "first" generation of immigrants who migrate as adults and the "second" generation of native-born persons of foreign parentage (Rumbaut, 2004). Rumbaut further classifies immigrants on a scale ranging from 1.25 to 1.75 based on age at arrival (the younger child being closer to 1.75 and the teenager closer to 1.25). However, information on age at time of immigration is often not available in large quantitative studies and thus using high school domicile allows for an age approximation. Age at time of immigration is important because younger immigrant children may relate more to the culture of their new home, while older immigrant children may have a greater connectedness to the prior culture. Additionally, younger immigrant children will have received the bulk of their education in the language of their adopted country.

This chapter uses examples from research on immigrant students to demonstrate that the use of a critical quantitative perspective can yield some important findings and implications. The critical quantitative dimension of research is needed "to demonstrate that for particular population groups, some widely accepted models and assumptions are inaccurate" (Stage, 2007, p. 10). A critical quantitative lens illuminates differences between native students and immigrant students, to better understand their expectations and outcomes as they pursue higher education.

Diversity of the Immigrant Population and the Rapid Pace of Change

Like the fable of the seven men who touched the elephant's trunk—one touched the trunk and thought it was a snake, a second touched the tail and thought it was a rope, and so on—a snapshot of immigrants in the United States is only a small part of the story. The immigrant population in earlier generations stemmed mainly from Europe, and today comes largely from Latin America and Asia, as shown in Figure 5.1.

Broadly, immigrant students are on average younger and more likely to live in poverty than their native student peers. They have less education and likely immigrated to the United States since 1990; half live in one of four states: California, New York, Texas, and Florida. But a more nuanced picture reveals the diversity of the immigrant population. While there are similarities among the new immigrants—they are young, often lacking in formal education, and living predominately in major cities—there are also differences (Teranishi, Suarez-Orozco, & Suarez-Orozco, 2011).

The student stories below are illustrative of the diversity in the immigrant population (data from Gambino & Gryn, 2011; Grieco et al., 2012).

Jessenia, a 26-year-old nursing student, is from the Dominican Republic and considers herself both Black and Hispanic. She completed her GED shortly after arriving in the United States. She hopes to bring her young daughter to New York once she completes her nursing degree at the community college.

Figure 5.1. U.S. Foreign-Born Population by Region of Birth, 2010

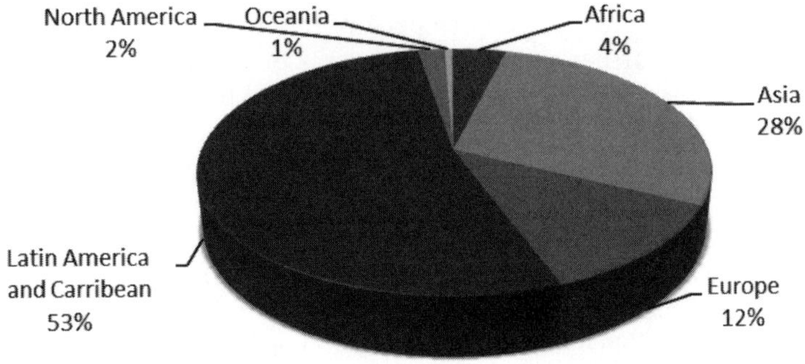

Note: Adapted from "The Foreign-Born Population in the United States: 2010," by E. M. Grieco, Y. D. Acosta, G. P. de la Cruz, C. Gambino, T. Gryn, L. J. Larsen, …., N. P. Walters, 2012, American Community Survey Reports No. ACS-19. U.S. Census Bureau.

In Caribbean immigrant households, one out of every four households is led by a woman with no husband present. Among Black immigrants from the Caribbean, the least educated are from the Dominican Republic, while the best educated are from the Bahamas. In the United States since 2000, Black immigrants from Africa have outpaced Black immigrants from the Caribbean.

Priyanka and Rakesh, newlyweds from India and graduate students living in Iowa, first came to the United States to attend college and stayed to pursue graduate degrees. Priyanka is pregnant and they are undecided about staying in the United States long term. Immigrant householders born in Asia were the most likely (63%) to be in a married-couple household. Nearly half of all Asian immigrants have completed a baccalaureate degree, compared to 28% of those native born and 27% of all immigrants. Of the 4.2 million foreign-born science and engineering bachelor's degree holders in the United States, 57% were born in Asia, 18% in India. In 2010, the highest proportions of foreign born with science and engineering degrees were found in "college towns."

Guadalupe was born in Mexico but immigrated illegally to the United States with her parents when she was a toddler. She recently graduated from a high school in East Los Angeles, and wanted to go away to college, but her illegal status made that impossible. She attends classes at a community college, works part-time, and helps care for her younger siblings. Her abuela, or grandmother, lives with the family. Her parents do not have high school degrees; her mother is a domestic worker and her father, a gardener. Mexican immigrant households have the largest average household size at 4.4 persons, and most (77%) have at least one child less than 18 years of age. Over 12% of family households were multigenerational. Sixty percent of Mexican immigrants have less than a high school degree. The poverty rate (28%) is highest for the foreign-born population born in Mexico (28%).

Figure 5.2. Foreign-Born Population and Percent of Total Population: 1970–2010

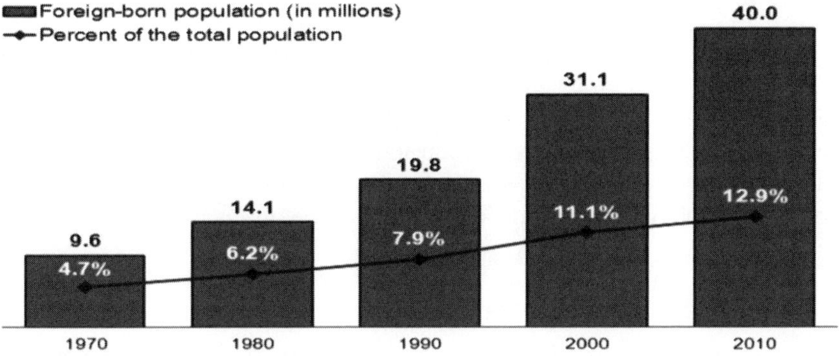

Note: Adapted from "The 'second great wave' of immigration: Growth of the foreign-born population since 1970," by E. M. Grieco, 2014, Random Samplings blog. U.S. Census Bureau.

Jack is from New Zealand, works for a yacht brokerage in Miami, and earns enough to live in a beach front condo. He is taking an engineering class at Miami-Dade because he knows that engineers are scarce in New Zealand and he hopes to return there in the future. The median income for foreign-born households from Oceania was $71,441, which exceeded the median income of the native-born and all other region-of-birth households.

Today, as seen in Figure 5.2, immigrants comprise approximately 13% of the total population, lower than the estimated 15% of the population near the start of the 20th century but a much higher absolute number as the U.S. population has grown. What is also important about the current immigrant population in the United States is the recency of their arrival. More than half the immigrants in the United States have arrived since 1990, a third as recently as 2000, and 17.4% since 2005. Also, because of their relative youth and fertility, recent immigrants and their children will have a large impact on both educational systems and the labor force in the coming years.

The Need for Research on Immigrant Students

Educating immigrants and their children is crucial. By 2030 immigrants, legal and illegal, are projected to account for 18% of the U.S. labor force (Lowell, 2006). As the U.S. economy has evolved into a "knowledge" economy with service jobs that demand technical and informational skills, more jobs than ever require postsecondary education. Additionally, numerous studies by the U.S. Department of Labor and others have shown that immigrants keep labor-intensive industries competitive and contribute to job growth (Anrig & Wang, 2004).

NEW DIRECTIONS FOR INSTITUTIONAL RESEARCH • DOI: 10.1002/ir

The gap between high school and college graduates' earnings has widened such that college graduates can expect to earn close to 60% more than high school graduates (NCES, 2007). If immigrants are going to be valued and contributing members of society, then access to and success in postsecondary education is a necessity, not a luxury. Insufficient education is one reason for high levels of immigrant poverty (50% higher than those native born) and a reason that a third of all immigrant-headed households rely on some form of welfare (Camarota, 2007). Given the economic ramifications, research on the education of immigrants and their children is crucial for policymakers to make informed decisions.

Immigrants in Higher Education

Despite the heterogeneity of the new immigrants, they often share both a common belief that education is important and a willingness to sacrifice in order for their children to achieve educational goals (Portes & Hao, 2004). In a study of immigrant children and their parents, when parents were asked "How do you get ahead in the United States?" the most frequent response was education; the children, when asked if education was important, overwhelmingly replied positively (Suarez-Orozco & Suarez-Orozco, 2001).

Unfortunately, some subpopulations of immigrants lack the academic preparation necessary for college, have limited resources, and need to gain English language skills, factors which combine to make applying to college a daunting process. Differences across immigrant groups (country of origin and education prior to arrival in the United States), however, can often be larger than differences in comparison to native students (Baum & Flores, 2011), suggesting the need for more studies of immigrant students as distinct from studies of racial/ethnic groups.

Educational Aspirations

Research has shown that educational expectations affect student performance and educational outcomes (Cheng & Starks, 2002; Museus & Hendel, 2005; Pascarella & Terenzini, 2005; Trusty, 2002), yet little research exists on the aspirations of one of the most rapidly growing student populations in higher education: immigrant students in the community college. Numerous studies exist for children of immigrants during their high school years (Portes & Hao, 2004; Suarez-Orozco & Suarez-Orozco, 2001; Wells, 2010) but not at the postsecondary level. Conway (2010) explored the educational aspirations of immigrant and native students in an urban community college, using Burton Clark's cooling-out theory as a framework. The study examined choices students make when applying to college and the extent to which students later change their aspirations. Clark (1960, 1980) suggested that community colleges, based on an assessment of a student's academic capabilities, redirect students away from a four-year transfer program and into a vocational track.

Conway's analysis revealed that immigrant students who were educated in U.S. high schools were more likely than other student groups (native students, native students with immigrant parents, and foreign high schooled immigrants) to aspire to a four-year degree and seek admission to a senior college rather than a community college. This finding supports previous research that shows immigrant students have higher aspirations (Brinbaum & Cebolla-Boado, 2007; Heath & Brinbaum, 2007; Jonsson & Rudolphi, 2010) and yet immigrants are more likely to attend community colleges (Teranishi et al., 2011) which may suggest that many immigrants attend community colleges not because it is their first choice but rather because they were redirected to a community college due to a lack of academic preparedness. Native students and the foreign high schooled immigrant students were the least likely to apply directly to a senior college. This may be because native students and their parents who are also native born are more aware of the requirements for admission to the senior colleges. The foreign high schooled students who were less likely to speak English, and who therefore may have been directed to the community college for ESL classes, may also be less likely to appreciate the differences in the U.S. educational hierarchy and perceived limitations attendant with starting at the community college. As a result, even though the foreign high schooled immigrant students were better prepared academically than the two groups of native students, as demonstrated by the proportion of students who needed no remedial coursework, the foreign high schooled immigrant students were still the least likely group to apply directly to a senior college. In addition, the foreign high schooled students were the least likely to be residents qualifying for financial aid, which might also have propelled them toward the community college where tuition is lower.

In several aspects, immigrant students were unlike their native student peers: they were more likely to enroll in a vocational or terminal degree (nontransfer) program and less likely to enroll in liberal arts, despite similarities in their stated desire to transfer to a baccalaureate program. Immigrant status was more likely to be a determining factor in the selection of a program than was race/ethnicity. Another facet of program choice that warrants further critical analysis is the relationship between math aptitude (immigrant students had better math scores than native students [Conway, 2009, 2010], a finding supported by national data [Vigdor, 2012]) and enrollment in nontransfer career programs which rely on strong math skills (computer science, nursing, and other health care fields as an example). The majority of community college students since the 1980s have enrolled in nondegree, short-term certificate tracks and nontransfer programs (Anderson, Alfonso, & Sun, 2006), and these findings suggest that larger enrollments of immigrant students may be fueling that trend.

NEW DIRECTIONS FOR INSTITUTIONAL RESEARCH • DOI: 10.1002/ir

College Persistence

Using a framework based on existing theoretical models of persistence, Conway (2009) examined the same four student groups (native students, native students with immigrant parents, U.S. high schooled immigrant students, and foreign high schooled immigrants). A critical quantitative lens was essential in that existing models of persistence did not factor immigrant status into the equation, a distinct student subgroup not considered by models which focused on differences by race/ethnicity.

Conway's model incorporated variables (including race/ethnicity, age, gender, SES, academic preparation, ESL, enrollment status) commonly found in other models and supported in the literature and added immigration status. The dependent variable, persistence, was measured as the number of real (nonremedial) credits completed as a proportion of the real credits attempted.

Multiple regression analysis revealed significant differences between the native student and immigrant student groups on three variables: full-/part-time status, remediation needs, and credit completion. Most students enrolled full-time, and switched to part-time status after the first year, although immigrants continued full-time to a greater extent than native students. Upon entry, 80% of the students in this sample needed some type of remediation. Native students needed more math remediation, and immigrants needed more reading or writing remediation, probably due to the fact that a greater proportion of immigrant students were ESL speakers. More than half of the immigrant students in the sample were ESL speakers, compared to 11% of the native students and 21% of the first-generation native students. A third of the total college freshman class spoke English as a second language. This ESL pattern is indicative of migratory patterns generally; native students are least likely to need ESL, followed in frequency by students born to immigrant parents, then by immigrant students who have lived here long enough to attend U.S. high school, and finally by the most recent group—immigrants who attended high school abroad.

ESL and immigrant status are closely related to ethnicity (Erisman & Looney, 2007; Lopez, Gonzalez-Barrera, & Patten, 2013; The New American Consumer, 2012). Erisman & Looney (2007) contend that Latino(a) immigrants are at a significant disadvantage in postsecondary educational attainment in general, compared with other immigrant groups. In 2003–2004, almost 75% of Latino(a) immigrant undergraduate students said that English was not their primary language, by far the highest percentage reported for any ethnic group. Even among those for whom English is a first language, Latino(a)s born in the United States to U.S.-born parents, 45% say they prefer to speak Spanish some of the time (Lopez et al., 2013; The New American Consumer, 2012).

However, ESL data, like much of the data for immigrant students, warrant further critical quantitative study because it is often based on static

New Directions for Institutional Research • DOI: 10.1002/ir

categories and broad generalizations (Noguera, 2004). For example, in 2009, 16% each of Hispanics and Asians spoke a non-English language at home and spoke English with difficulty (Aud et al., 2011), but within these broad groups there were large differences. Among Asians, for example, three fourths of Filipino households said they spoke only English at home or spoke English very well, a proportion which dropped to 37.5% among Vietnamese households (Teranishi, 2007).

Another area warranting more critical analysis is the gender gap as it relates to immigrant students. While overall females participate and persist in education at higher rates than their male counterparts (Aud, Fox, & KewalRamani, 2010; Aud et al., 2011), enrollment by women students was lowest among native students with immigrant parents (Conway, 2009, 2010). This is consistent with research that shows that cultural barriers in regard to gender roles may hinder educational persistence, such as the "macho" attitude cited in many Latin cultures (Cejda & Stick, 2008), but inconsistent with broader trends in female enrollment and suggests a need for analysis of particular subgroups when examining female students.

Research shows that lacking a high school diploma, attending part-time, having dependents, having lower academic aspirations, and being less well prepared academically are all characteristics of the broad group of Hispanic students and characteristics which, independent of being Hispanic, contribute to lack of persistence (Adelman, 2005, 2006; NCES, 2002; Schuetze & Slowey, 2002). However, research on the subgroup of Hispanic students classified by their immigrant status found that Hispanic ethnicity was significant in contributing to a lack of credit completion only for the immigrant students who attended U.S. high schools (Conway, 2009). The U.S. high schooled immigrant student was at the greatest disadvantage when trying to combine language proficiency and subject mastery in order to prepare for college. The two groups of native students received their academic preparation (high school) in English, their native language. The foreign high schooled immigrant student also learned their subject matter in their native language prior to migration. This suggests the importance of identifying students not simply by their ESL status but also to identify the language in which they received their academic preparation.

The Need for Critical Research

Future quantitative analysis should focus on narrow groups of students (e.g., female first-generation immigrants from China who speak English) rather than broad groups (e.g., Asians, females, etc.) which have been studied in the past. Further, research should examine subgroups by immigrant generation, country of origin, English language ability, as well as the conditions under which immigration occurs, and the conditions under which immigrants find themselves upon arrival. A student, for example, who resides in an ethnic enclave of other immigrants from his/her country of origin, will have a very different experience from a student who lives in a truly "foreign" environment. For example, national graduation rates at community colleges are about equal for Hispanic (32.8%) and White (32%) students; however, there are large state-by-state differences (e.g., just over 50% of Hispanics in community colleges in Florida earn a degree within three years but in New York, the Hispanic graduation rate is only 17% [Liu, 2011]). These differences may be due to ethnicity (Cubans arriving with more education than Dominicans for example), environmental factors (residing in a community that is politically stronger and provides greater access to resources), or personal circumstance (living alone vs. among family). To the extent improved techniques for data collection and/or analysis allow a narrower focus, we can better address student needs and find solutions.

Researchers must remain attentive to limitations of a quantitative approach. Identifying, for example, that students are foreign-born and that English is their second language may not fully identify students with ESL needs. For instance, in some traditionally immigrant neighborhoods of New York City, the majority of residents, both immigrants and others in their household, speak a language other than English at home, either from necessity or desire, suggesting that native-born students might also benefit from supplemental English language instruction (Lobo & Salvo, 2004; Lopez et al., 2013; The New American Consumer, 2012). Conversely, an immigrant student with strong academic preparation, but limited English language skills, might be misdirected into remedial coursework or toward vocational degree choices, which may not fulfill the student's full potential.

The critical analysis of data provides a starting point for discussions that question and extend existing frameworks and encourage further research of subpopulations of immigrant students from both a quantitative and a qualitative perspective. Policy makers and institutional decision makers should consider immigrant status as a factor when planning for, requesting, and allocating limited resources because immigrant students are changing the educational landscape. Researchers need to learn more about specific subgroups (e.g., French-speaking African immigrants) in order to identify the best types of student support services, but national data is not presently available and institutional data may be limited. Institutional decision makers should consider combining both research efforts and resource allocation for immigrant student groups. A good example of this type of effort is the Community College Consortium for Immigrant Education, a group of 23 colleges, which seeks to generate awareness on the role of community colleges in educating immigrant students and to expand programs and services for these students. Research on immigrant students is also essential if institutional decision makers are going to contribute to the municipal and national debates on immigrant education policy in a concerted unified way that will maximize returns to higher education students and institutions.

References

Adelman, C. (2005). *Moving into town—and moving on: The community college in the lives of traditional-age students.* Washington, DC: U.S. Department of Education.

Adelman, C. (2006). *The toolbox revisited. Paths to degree completion from high school through college.* Washington, DC: U.S. Department of Education.

Anderson, G., Alfonso, M., & Sun, J. C. (2006). Rethinking cooling out at public community colleges: An examination of fiscal and demographic trends in higher education and the rise of statewide articulation agreements. *Teachers College Record, 108*(3), 422–451.

Anrig, G., Jr., & Wang, T. A. (2004). *Immigration, jobs and the new economy.* Washington, DC: The Century Foundation.

Armstrong, D. M., & Ortman, J. M. (2013, April 11–13). *Projecting the foreign-born population in the United States: 2012 to 2060.* Population Division, U.S. Census Bureau. Paper presented at the annual meeting of the Population Association of America, New Orleans, LA. Retrieved from http://paa2013.princeton.edu/papers/130561

Aud, S., Fox, M., & KewalRamani, A. (2010). *Status and trends in the education of racial and ethnic groups* (NCES 2010-015). U.S. Department of Education, National Center for Education Statistics. Washington, DC: U.S. Government Printing Office.

Aud, S., Hussar, W., Kena, G., Bianco, K., Frohlich, L., Kemp, J., & Tahan, K. (2011). *The condition of education 2011* (NCES 2011-033). U.S. Department of Education, National Center for Education Statistics. Washington, DC: U.S. Government Printing Office.

Baum, S., & Flores, S. M. (2011). Higher education and children in immigrant families. *Future Child, Spring, 21*(1), 171–193.

Brinbaum, Y., & Cebolla-Boado, H. (2007). The school careers of ethnic minority youth in France: Success or disillusion? *Ethnicities, 7*(3), 445–474.

Camarota, S. A. (2007). *Immigrants in the United States, 2007: A profile of America's foreign-born population.* Washington, DC: Center for Immigration Studies. Retrieved from http://www.cis.org/articles/2007/back1007.html

Camarota, S. A., & Zeigler, K. (2009). *A shifting tide: Recent trends in the illegal immigrant population.* Center for Immigration Studies. Retrieved from http://cis.org/IllegalImmigration-ShiftingTide

Cejda, B. D., & Stick, S. L. (2008). *Paths to the baccalaureate. A study of transfer and native students at a Hispanic-Serving Institution.* Retrieved from http://www.tgslc.org/pdf/PathstotheBaccalaureate.pdf

Cheng, S., & Starks, B. (2002). Racial differences in the effects of significant others on students' educational expectations. *Sociology of Education, 75*(4), 306–327.

Clark, B. R. (1960). The cooling-out function in higher education. *The American Journal of Sociology, 65*, 569–576.

Clark, B. R. (1980). The "cooling-out" function revisited. In G. B. Vaughan (Ed.), *New Directions for Community Colleges: No. 32. Questioning the community college role* (pp. 15–31). San Francisco, CA: Jossey-Bass.

Conway, K. M. (2009). Exploring persistence of immigrant and native students in an urban community college. *Review of Higher Education, 32*(3), 321–352.

Conway, K. M. (2010). Educational aspirations in an urban community college: Differences between immigrant and native student groups. *Community College Review, 37*(3), 209–242.

Erisman, W., & Looney, S. (2007). *Opening the door to the American dream: Increasing higher education access and success for immigrants. A report by the Institute for Higher Education Policy.* Retrieved from http://www.dsa.csupomona.edu/ab540/files/OpeningTheDoor_8059.pdf

Gambino, C., & Gryn, T. (2011). *The foreign born with science and engineering degrees: 2010* (American Community Survey Reports No. ACSBR/10-06). U.S. Census Bureau. Retrieved from http://www.census.gov/prod/2011pubs/acsbr10-06.pdf

Grieco, E. M. (2014). *The "second great wave" of immigration: Growth of the foreign-born population since 1970.* U.S. Census Bureau, Random Samplings blog. Retrieved from http://blogs.census.gov/2014/02/26/the-second-great-wave-of-immigration-growth-of-the-foreign-born-population-since-1970/

Grieco, E. M., Acosta, Y. D., de la Cruz, G. P., Gambino, C., Gryn, T., Larsen, L. J., ..., Walters, N. P. (2012). *The foreign-born population in the United States: 2010* (American Community Survey Reports No. ACS-19). U.S. Census Bureau. Retrieved from http://www.census.gov/prod/2012pubs/acs-19.pdf

Heath, A., & Brinbaum, Y. (2007). Explaining ethnic inequalities in educational attainment. *Ethnicities, 7*(3), 291–305.

Jonsson, J. O., & Rudolphi, F. (2010). Weak performance—Strong determination: School achievement and educational choice among children of immigrants in Sweden. *European Sociological Review, 27*(4), 487–508.

Liu, M. (2011, July). *Trends in Latino college access and success.* National Conference of State Legislatures. Retrieved from http://www.ncsl.org/documents/educ/trendsinlatinosuccess.pdf

Lobo, A. P., & Salvo, J. J. (2004). *The newest New Yorkers* (No. NYC DCP 04-09). New York: NYC Dept. of City Planning.

Lopez, M. H., Gonzalez-Barrera, A., & Patten, E. (2013). *Closing the digital divide: Latinos and technology adoption.* Pew Research Hispanic Center. Retrieved from http://www.pewhispanic.org/2013/03/07/closing-the-digital-divide-latinos-and-technology-adoption/

Lowell, B. L. (2006, July). *Immigration and labor force trends: The future, past and present* (No. 17). Washington, DC: Migration Policy Institute.

Museus, S. D., & Hendel, D. D. (2005). Test scores, self-efficacy, and the educational plans of first-year college students. *Higher Education in Review, 2*, 63–88.

National Center for Education Statistics (NCES). (2002). *Findings from the condition of education: Non-traditional undergraduates.* Retrieved from http://nces.ed.gov/pubs2002/2002012.pdf

National Center for Education Statistics (NCES). (2007). *The condition of education 2007* (NCES 2007–064). Washington, DC: U.S. Department of Education.

The New American Consumer. (2012). *The new American consumer: State of the Hispanic consumer marketplace. Experian marketing services.* Retrieved from http://ahaa.org/downloads/Research/marketig-services-hispanic-demographic-report-11-2012.pdf

Noguera, P. A. (2004). Social capital and the education of immigrant students: Categories and generalizations. *Sociology of Education, 77*, 180–183.

Pascarella, E. T., & Terenzini, P. T. (2005). *How college affects students, Vol. 2. A third decade of research.* San Francisco, CA: Jossey-Bass.

Patten, E. (2012). *Statistical portrait of the foreign-born population in the United States, 2010.* Washington, DC: Pew Hispanic Center. Retrieved from http://www.pewhispanic.org/2012/02/21/statistical-portrait-of-the-foreign-born-population-in-the-united-states-2010/#26

Perna, L. W. (2000). Differences in the decision to attend college among African Americans, Hispanics and Whites. *The Journal of Higher Education, 71*(2), 117–141.

Perna, L. W., Li, C., Walsh, E., & Raible, S. (2010). The status of equity for Hispanics in public higher education in Florida and Texas. *Journal of Hispanic Higher Education, 9*(2), 145–166.

Perna, L. W., & Titus, M. (2005). The relationship between parental involvement as social capital and college enrollment: An examination of racial/ethnic group differences. *Journal of Higher Education, 76*, 485–518.

Portes, A., & Hao, L. (2004). The schooling of children of immigrants: Contextual effects on the educational attainment of the second generation. *PNAS, National Academy of Sciences, 101*(33), 11920–11927.

Rendon, L. I., Jalomo, R. E., & Nora, A. (2000). Theoretical considerations in the study of minority student retention in higher education. In J. M. Braxton (Ed.), *Reworking the student departure puzzle* (pp. 127–156). Nashville, TN: Vanderbilt University Press.

Rumbaut, R. G. (2004). Ages, life stages, and generational cohorts: Decomposing the immigrant first and second generations in the United States. *International Migration Review, 38*, 1160–1205.

Schuetze, H. G., & Slowey, M. (2002). Participation and exclusion: A comparison analysis of non-traditional students and lifelong learners in higher education. *Higher Education, 44*(3–4), 309–327.

Stage, F. K. (2007). Answering critical questions using quantitative data. In F. K. Stage (Ed.), *New Directions for Institutional Research: No. 133. Using quantitative data to answer critical questions* (pp. 5–16). San Francisco, CA: Jossey-Bass.

Staklis, S., Horn, L., & Soldner, M. (2012). *New Americans in postsecondary education. A profile of immigrant and second-generation American undergraduates* (NCES 2012-213). Washington, DC: National Center for Education Statistics, U.S. Department of Education. Retrieved from http://nces.ed.gov/pubs2012/2012213.pdf

Suarez-Orozco, C., & Suarez-Orozco, M. M. (2001). *Children of immigrants*. Cambridge, MA: Harvard University Press.

Teranishi, R. T. (2002). "Raced" perspectives on college opportunity: Examining Asian Americans through critical race theory. *Equity and Excellence in Education, 35*(2), 144–154.

Teranishi, R. T. (2007). Race, ethnicity and higher education policy: The use of critical quantitative research. In F. K. Stage (Ed.), *New Directions for Institutional Research: No. 133. Using quantitative data to answer critical questions* (pp. 37–49). San Francisco, CA: Jossey-Bass.

Teranishi, R. T., Suarez-Orozco, C., & Suarez-Orozco, M. (2011). Immigrants in community colleges. *Future of Children, 21*(1), 153–169.

Trusty, J. (2002). African Americans' educational expectations: Longitudinal causal models for women and men. *Journal of Counseling and Development, 80*, 332–345.

Vigdor, J. L. (2012). *Solving America's mathematics education problem*. American Enterprise Institute. Retrieved from http://www.aei.org/papers/education/k-12/solving-americas-mathematics-education-problem/

Wells, R. (2010). Children of immigrants and educational expectations: The roles of school composition. *Teachers College Record, 112*(6), 1679–1704.

KATHERINE M. CONWAY *is a professor of business at Borough of Manhattan Community College, City University of New York.*

6

Numbers of students of color enrolling in higher educational institutions is expected to increase across all racial groups. With continued increases in minority enrollments, minority-serving institutions have and will continue to play a major role in educating student of color. A large national data set was used to examine the numbers of bachelor's degrees awarded to students by minority-serving institutions, predominantly minority institutions, and predominantly white institutions. The analysis indicates that minority-serving institutions are important producers of students of color who earn bachelor's degrees.

Minority-Serving Institutions and the Education of U.S. Underrepresented Students

Ginelle John, Frances K. Stage

If the United States intends to meet its goal of having the highest college degree attainment rates in the world by 2020 (The White House, 2013), attention must be given to Minority-Serving Institutions (MSIs). MSIs educate a large percentage of underrepresented minority and low-income students and play a vital role in educating students of color (Gasman, Baez, & Turner, 2008; Li, 2007). According to the 2013 National Center for Education Statistics (NCES) report, the number of minority students attending high educational institutions is expected to increase significantly. While the rate of White students enrolling in college is expected to increase 4% between 2010 and 2021, enrollment is expected to increase at least 20% for Black and Asian students and 42% for Hispanic students (U.S. Department of Education, National Center of Education Statistics [NCES], 2013b). In the past decade, increasing numbers of students have entered college, yet college attainment rates have not changed, prompting a shift in focus from attendance to completion (U.S. Department of Education, 2012).

Institutions designated as MSIs by the U.S. Department of Education have access to federal funds and other resources to support their students

New Directions for Institutional Research, no. 158 © 2014 Wiley Periodicals, Inc.
Published online in Wiley Online Library (wileyonlinelibrary.com) • DOI: 10.1002/ir.20046

and communities (U.S. Department of the Interior, 2013). These institutions share a common goal of educating underrepresented students, providing cultural academic programs, and serving their communities (Baez, Gasman, & Turner, 2008). Additionally, MSIs have demonstrated the ability to graduate underrepresented minority college students at rates that exceed those of predominantly White populations (Stage, Lundy-Wagner, & John, 2012).

This chapter employs a critical quantitative approach to learn more about the contexts within which underrepresented students of color enter and experience the process of postsecondary education. In Chapter 1 of this volume, Stage and Wells enjoin researchers "to conduct culturally relevant research by studying institutions and people in context" (p. 3). We directed our research in a way that examined the institutional contexts within which underrepresented students study. We began by viewing existing literature examining the history and role of MSIs, and the successes and challenges these institutions face. We then used data from a large national data set to examine the numbers of bachelor's degrees awarded to underrepresented students by three types of institutions: MSIs, predominantly minority institutions (PMIs), and predominantly White institutions (PWIs). PMIs included predominantly minority institutions (PMIs) whose minority enrollment exceeded 50% of an institution's total enrollment but were not federally designated as an MSI (U.S. Department of Education, 2013). The use of national data provides a broader context for understanding the roles played by various types of institutions. We begin with a brief discussion of these institutional types.

History and Role of Minority-Serving Institutions

Federally designated MSIs include Historically Black Colleges and Universities (HBCUs), Hispanic-Serving Institutions (HSIs), Tribal Colleges and Universities (TCUs), and Asian American and Native American Pacific Islander-Serving Institutions (AANAPISIs). HBCUs are the oldest MSIs and were created to educate Black students. Initially, these institutions provided religious education to Black youths and basic skills training to emancipated slaves after the Civil War. However, a number of HBCUs were founded in the later 19th century as a result of segregation policies that prevented Black students from attending institutions that educated White students (Merisotis & McCarthy, 2005; O'Brien & Zudak, 1998; Redd, 1998). Today, over 100 HBCUs represent only 3% of all colleges and universities in the country, yet they enroll 16% of Black students (Harmon, 2012). HBCUs are diverse in type, including two- and four-year, public and private, urban and rural, and open and selective college admissions (Gasman, 2013).

HSIs educate a large percentage of students who self-identify as Hispanic or Latino (Laden, 2004). While many HSIs were historically PWIs, economic and demographic changes resulted in a number of these institutions enrolling large numbers of underrepresented and low-income students (Laden, 2004; Mercer & Stedman, 2008). Although Hispanics are one of the fastest growing minority populations in the United States, their enrollment in colleges lags behind their population growth (Brown & Santiago, 2004). Over 200 institutions are described as "emerging" HSIs. While not officially designated as HSIs, many will soon qualify as an HSI due to the number of Hispanic students enrolling in these institutions (Excelencia in Education, 2012/2013; Nunez & Elizondo, 2012).

While four-year HSIs exist, the majority are public community colleges (Benítez, 1998; Brown & Santiago, 2004). For an academic institution to qualify as an HSI it must have 25% Hispanic full-time equivalent enrollment, 50% of whom must be low income (Contreras, Malcom, & Bensimon, 2008). Over 250 institutions meet the HSI designation criteria. Additionally, this is one of the fastest growing sectors of MSIs. In the early 1990s, fewer than two dozen colleges identified as Hispanic-serving. Today, over 400 institutions of higher education identify as servers of significant numbers of Hispanic students (Hispanic Association of Colleges and Universities, 2014). While these institutions enroll over 40% of all Hispanic students, in number they represent less than 5% of all postsecondary institutions (Harmon, 2012).

TCUs provide college access primarily to American Indian students. Although Native Americans were granted access to higher education institutions throughout America's higher education history, the goal was not to empower them, but to convert them to the ways of the colonists (Guillory & Ward, 2008). The direction of educating American Indian students changed in the 1960s as a result of the American Indian Movement. Not only was the first TCU created during that decade, the mission of these institutions was to provide culturally based education to Native Americans (Griffin & Hurtado, 2011). These institutions accomplish this by providing training for the workforce, providing postsecondary education, preserving culture and language, and promoting local economic development (Merisotis & McCarthy, 2005).

Enrollment at TCUs has expanded rapidly from only 2100 American Indians enrolled in 1982. As the growth continues many TCUs struggle to meet the enrollment demand (Brayboy, Fann, Castagno, & Solyom, 2012; Shotton, Lowe & Waterman, 2013). Today, over 30 TCUs exist and enroll students from over 250 tribal nations (Griffin & Hurtado, 2011). The majority of TCUs are two-year community colleges enrolling close to 20% of Native American college students, though representing less than 1% of all postsecondary institutions (Harmon, 2012; Merisotis & McCarthy, 2005; O'Brien & Zudak, 1998).

In 2008, the federal government created the AANAPISIs federal program. This program made it possible for institutions with at least 10% of Asian American and Pacific Islander (AAPI) students, a significant percentage of low-income students, and lower than average educational expenditure per student to compete for federal grants (National Commission on Asian American and Pacific Islander Research in Education, 2012). AANAPISIs recognize the unique challenges AAPI students face in college and are committed to increasing the retention rates of AAPI and low-income students (Teranishi, 2012). In addition, AANAPISIs focus on improving institutions' academic quality and institutional and fiscal management (Harmon, 2012; U.S. Department of Education, 2012). There are two- and four-year public AANAPISI institutions and the majority are located on the East and West coasts.

Successes and Challenges

Research has indicated that one of the benefits of attending an MSI is its supportive environment. MSIs have been shown to provide a nurturing, supportive environment that maintains the underrepresented minority culture, and relative freedom from racial discrimination (Brown, 2003; Gasman et al., 2008). Additionally, for students new to college, MSIs provide an environment comparatively rich in role models among faculty and staff, as well as upper class students. Hurtado, Alvarez, Guillermo-Wann, Cuellar, and Arellano (2012) describe the ways that aspects of campus climate are related to diverse students' comfort, integration, and ultimate success in college study. As a result of the nurturing and encouraging aspects of institutions with large numbers of diverse students, a supportive milieu is provided that engenders academic success for underrepresented students (Stage et al., 2012).

MSIs pride themselves in providing students of color access to higher education. The majority of students attending MSIs receive financial assistance; in fact, close to 100% of Black and Native American students attending MSIs are eligible for need-based aid (Gasman et al., 2008). In addition, because Black and Latino students are more likely to attend poorly funded secondary schools, they are more likely than their White counterparts to be less academically prepared for college and to require developmental education courses (Harmon, 2012; Southern Education Foundation, 2011). Due to economic reasons and lack of academic preparation, attending an MSI may be a student of color's only opportunity to further their postsecondary education. MSIs also often provide the education of first-generation college-bound students, particularly those who lacked family members to provide college preparation guidance during their secondary education.

A positive factor related to attending MSIs is their contribution to producing graduates in important fields such as science, technology, engineering, and math (Stage & Hubbard, 2009; Stage, John, & Hubbard, 2011; Stage et al., 2012), as well as teaching. Research has shown that two- and four-year MSIs awarded a greater proportion of certificate, associate's, and baccalaureate degrees to students of color compared to their overall representation. In addition, MSIs produce a substantial number of teachers. Over 40% of African-American and Latino students and 12% of Native Americans earn their bachelor's degree in teaching from an MSI (Harmon, 2012).

A great challenge for MSIs is lack of funding and resources. MSIs generally serve lower socioeconomic students who rely on financial assistance to help defray the cost of tuition. Although there are some large and wealthy MSIs, many of these institutions are faced with great financial burdens (Baez et al., 2008). Due to lack of funding, many schools find it difficult to provide scholarship monies to students, making it challenging for them to attract and recruit academically strong students. Lack of funding also makes it difficult for these institutions to compete for top faculty, update facilities, establish substantial endowments, and maintain and update technological infrastructures (Bridges, Cambridge, Kuh, & Hawthorne Leegwater, 2005; Cunningham & Parker, 1998; Hurtado et al., 2012; Redd, 1998).

Another challenge facing MSIs is low graduation rates. Many, with open admissions policies, enroll large numbers of incoming students who are underprepared for college level work, and who require developmental coursework, programs, and advising (Southern Education Foundation, 2011). Students attending these institutions are at a greater risk of experiencing academic difficulties due to poor academic preparation and lack of financial assistance, obstacles that would make it difficult for any student to complete college (Mercer & Stedman, 2008). Additionally, two-year institutions typically have lower success rates than four-year institutions. Many PMIs and MSIs, particularly HSIs and TCUs, are two-year institutions. When examining enrollment and success rates these factors play an important role in the analysis.

The United States now lags behind countries like Canada and China in producing college graduates (The White House, 2013). Given the large numbers of students of color attending MSIs, the successes of students at these institutions will significantly impact efforts to meet the country's goals of increasing educational attainment rates (Harmon, 2012; Kim & Conrad, 2006; Southern Education Foundation, 2011). Below we describe the relative production of bachelor's degrees for college students of all races for MSIs, PMIs, and PWIs.

Methods

To identify the relative contributions of four-year MSIs, PMIs, and PWIs on the awarding of bachelor's degrees to students of color, we conducted a descriptive quantitative analysis of a cohort of baccalaureate degree awardees from all four-year U.S. institutions in one calendar year. Baccalaureate degree awardees were identified using Integrated Postsecondary Education Data System (IPEDS) from the Institute of Education Sciences on the NCES website (U.S. Department of Education, NCES, 2013a).

IPEDS consists of annual surveys of higher education institutions collected by the U.S. Department of Education, NCES (2013a). These surveys include data in several categories (i.e., institutional characteristics, enrollment and completion rates, financial aid, finance, and staffing) from all postsecondary institutions receiving federal student aid. We used the institutional characteristics data to identify all institutions awarding baccalaureate degrees that were also designated MSIs (AANAPISIs, HSIs, HBCUs, and TCUs) and PMIs for 2010–2011. The completion data used in this study included information on the number of degrees conferred by program, award level, race/ethnicity, and gender from July 1, 2010, to June 30, 2011.

IPEDS was used to identify four-year public and private not-for-profit institutions that granted bachelor's degrees in the 2011 data collection year. Institutions not located within the 50 U.S. states were excluded from the analysis. To identify the MSI institutions, we used the United States Department of Education *Lists of Postsecondary Institutions Enrolling Populations with Significant Percentages of Minority Students* (U.S. Department of Education, 2013). We designated as MSIs four-year institutions that were awarded MSI grants from the Office of Postsecondary Education (OPE) from 2006 to the present.

Findings

Table 6.1 reports the numbers and percentages of bachelor's degree recipients at MSIs, PMIs, and PWIs by race. Between July 2010 and June 2011, 1,845 colleges and universities awarded approximately 1.4 million bachelor's degrees. Twenty-seven percent (390,169) of those were awarded to underrepresented minority students. At MSIs, students of color (American Indian, Asian, Black, Latino, and Native Hawaiian) earned 65% of the bachelor's degrees awarded compared to 35% earned by White students. At PMIs, the respective numbers were 67% of the bachelor's degrees awarded to students of color compared with 33% for White students. Finally, students of color attending PWIs earned 22% of bachelor degrees awarded, while White students attending PWIs earned 78% of the total.

Comparing by institutional type, Latino students earned 29% of bachelor's degrees at MSIs, 20% at PMIs, and just 7% at PWIs. For Black students, the percentages of bachelor's degree at MSIs, PMIs, and PWIs were 24%, 32%, and 8%, respectively. Asian students earned 11% of four-year degrees at MSIs, 11% at PMIs, and 7% at PWIs. However, American Indians and Native Hawaiians earned 1% and 0.36% of bachelor's degree at MSIs. American Indians and Native Hawaiians each earned 2% four-year degrees at PMIs. Finally, both groups earned less than 1% of the bachelor's degrees awarded at PWIs (0.66% and 0.19%, respectively).

Table 6.2 presents the number and percentages of bachelor's degrees by race awarded by four-year MSIs ($N = 141$), PMIs ($N = 79$), and PWIs ($N = 1625$). While MSIs represent only 8% of four-year institutions awarding

Table 6.1. Number of Bachelor's Degrees by Institution Type and Race July 1, 2010, to June 30, 2011*

	American Indian Completion 11	Asian Completion 11	Black Completion 11	Latino Completion 11	Native Hawaiian Completion 11	White Completion 11	Total** Completion 11
MSI (N = 141)	1,153	14,006	31,705	38,499	470	45,874	131,707
	0.88%	10.63%	24.07%	29.23%	0.36%	34.83%	
PMI (N = 79)	768	3,804	11,109	6,942	597	11,400	34,620
	2.22%	10.99%	32.09%	20.05%	1.72%	32.93%	
PWI (N = 1625)	8,358	87,341	96,932	86,086	2,399	988,932	1,270,048
	0.66%	6.88%	7.63%	6.78%	0.19%	77.87%	
Total	10,279	105,151	139,746	131,527	3,466	1,046,206	1,436,375

*Data source: National Center for Education Statistics' Integrated Postsecondary Education Data System (IPEDS). Awards/degrees conferred by program (CIP), award level, race/ethnicity, and gender: July 1, 2010, to June 30, 2011.

**Total: The totals do not include students who self-identified as two or more races, other, or nonresident alien.

Table 6.2. Number and Percentage of Bachelor's Degrees by Race at MSIs, PMIs, and PWIs*

	Number of Bach Total	Number of Bach (MSI)	Bach (%) (MSI)	Number of Bach (PMI)	Bach (%) (PMI)	Number of Bach (PWI)	Bach (%) (PWI)
American Indian	10,279	1,153	11.22	768	7.47	8,358	81.31
Asian	105,151	14,006	13.32	3,804	3.62	87,341	83.06
Black	139,746	31,705	22.69	11,109	7.95	96,932	69.36
Latino	131,527	38,499	29.27	6,942	5.28	86,086	65.45
Native Hawaiian	3,466	470	13.56	597	17.22	2,399	69.22
Underrepresented student total	390,169	85,833	22.00	23,220	5.95	281,116	72.05
White	1,046,206	45,874	4.38	11,400	1.09	988,932	94.53
Total	1,436,375	131,707		34,620		1,270,048	

*Data source: National Center for Education Statistics' Integrated Postsecondary Education Data System (IPEDS). Awards/degrees conferred by program (CIP), award level, race/ethnicity, and gender: July 1, 2010 to June 30, 2011.

bachelor's degrees, in most cases they awarded percentages of bachelor's degrees far exceeding 8% for students of color. Twenty-nine percent of Latino students earned their bachelor's degrees at MSIs. Similarly, 23% of Black students, 14% of Native Hawaiian students, 13% of Asian students, and 11% of American Indians earned bachelor's degrees at MSIs. PMIs represent a smaller percentage of institutions awarding four-year degrees (4%) and the percentages they awarded to students of color were smaller as well but exceeded their percentage of institutions offering degrees. PMI awarded 17% of the bachelor's degrees earned by Native Hawaiian students. Eight percent of Black students, 7% of American Indians, and 5% of Latino students earned their bachelor's degrees at PMIs. However, only 4% of Asian students earned bachelor's degrees at PMIs. White students earned 4% of the bachelor's degrees awarded at MSIs, 1% at PMIs, and 95% of the degrees at PWIs.

In summary, MSIs and PMIs together represented only 220 or 12%, of the 1,845 institutions studied. Nevertheless, when numbers of students were totaled across those two groups, MSIs and PMIs awarded 28% (109,053) of the total bachelor's degrees (390,169) to underrepresented students. This is despite the fact that MSIs and PMIs generally have lower average enrollments than PWIs and many are open admission institutions. Clearly, these institutions are important for the success of underrepresented college students in the United States. While PWIs represented 88% of all institutions awarding bachelor's degree, they awarded 72% of the degrees earned by students of color. For researchers examining enrollments and outcomes for college students, focusing on different types of colleges, particularly MSIs and PMIs, may provide a greater understanding of factors leading to success for underrepresented students.

Conclusion

In this chapter we used a critical quantitative approach to learn more about the institutional contexts within which underrepresented students are able to succeed. We began by viewing existing literature examining the history and role of MSIs, and the successes and challenges these institutions face. We then used data from a large national data set to examine the numbers of bachelor's degrees awarded to underrepresented students by three types of institutions: MSIs, PMIs, and PWIs. The use of national data provides a broader context for understanding the roles played by various types of institutions.

While MSIs and PMIs are often open enrollment institutions enrolling relatively small numbers of students, they are important and impressive producers of bachelor's degrees for students of color. Studies focusing on baccalaureate origins of students examine institutions as the unit of analysis, comparing them in terms of the success of their baccalaureate graduates (Stage & Hubbard, 2009). Baccalaureate studies typically result in a listing of particular institutions that are successful in producing relatively large numbers of graduates who go on to succeed in some way. Other work focuses on specific types of MSIs and the role they play in underrepresented college student success (Contreras et al., 2008; Palmer, Davis, & Hilton, 2009). The research reported in this study focused on a national view of the role, in the aggregate, that MSIs play in the success of the undergraduate majors.

MSIs and PMIs represent a relatively small number of the thousands of postsecondary education institutions in the United States. Though small in number, they provide an environment for budding scholars, and particularly for underrepresented students seeking college education. Fully 28% of underrepresented graduates in 2011 earned bachelor's degrees at MSIs and PMIs. MSIs have a history of success in providing a college education to students of color, but the focus is usually on HBCUs or HSIs. AANAPISIs, TCUs, and increasingly PMIs play an important role in educating diverse students. An exception to these numbers was noted for the Native American and Native Hawaiian students. In this study and others these students have very low rates of college graduation relative to their population percentage. For many underrepresented students, education at a large MSI provides an option for education at a campus with a cultural climate that differs significantly from large impersonal PWIs. Unfortunately, many Native American and Native Hawaiian students live far from large MSIs. And although relatively large numbers of Native Americans attend TCUs, the number of those institutions is small and many of them are two-year colleges.

This research supports existing literature on MSIs and PMIs and the production of underrepresented undergraduates earning college degrees. Findings suggest that the MSIs as well as PMIs in this study not only produced a considerable number of underrepresented bachelor's degree recipients, but that bachelor's degree production for designated MSIs and PMIs and their respective ethnic/racial groups far exceeded the proportions represented by those institutions. We expect that future study will delve more deeply so we learn more about the contexts of these institutions. This was an exploratory study; perhaps if relative size of the institutions have been taken into account, the importance of this small number of MSIs and PMIs in the production of bachelor's degrees for underrepresented students might have been even more dramatic. For the future factors such as relative size, institutional selectivity, and their relationships to student success might be explored. Additionally, given the uneven distribution of college participation by gender, we might be able to learn more about institutional contexts that lead to greater success for male students.

References

Baez, B., Gasman, M., & Turner, C. (2008). On minority-serving institutions. In M. Gasman, B. Baez, & C. Turner (Eds.), *Understanding minority-serving institutions* (pp. 3–17). Albany, NY: State University of New York Press.

Benítez, M. (1998). Hispanic-Serving Institutions: Challenges and opportunities. In J. P. Merisotis & C. T. O'Brien (Eds.), *Minority-serving institutions: Distinct purposes, common goals* (pp. 57–68). San Francisco, CA: Jossey-Bass.

Brayboy, B. M. J., Fann, A. J., Castagno, A. E., & Solyom, J. A. (2012). Postsecondary education for American Indian and Alaska Natives: Higher education for nation building and self-determination. *ASHE Higher Education Report, 37*(5), 1–154.

Bridges, B. K., Cambridge, B., Kuh, G. D., & Hawthorne Leegwater, L. (2005, Spring). Student engagement at minority-serving institutions: Emerging lessons from the BEAMS project. In G. H. Gaither (Ed.), *New Directions for Institutional Research: No. 125. What works: Achieving success in minority retention* (pp. 25–43). San Francisco, CA: Jossey-Bass.

Brown, D. (2003). Tribal colleges: Playing a key role in the transition from secondary to postsecondary education for American Indian students. *Journal of American Indian Education, 42*(1), 36–45.

Brown, E. E., & Santiago, D. (2004). Latino students gravitate toward HSIs. *Hispanic Outlook in Higher Education, 15*(7), 21.

Contreras, F. E., Malcom, L. E., & Bensimon, E. M. (2008). Hispanic-Serving Institutions: Closeted identity and the production of equitable outcomes for Latino/a students. In M. Gasman, B. Baez, & C. Turner (Eds.), *Interdisciplinary approaches to understanding minority-serving institutions* (pp. 71–90). Albany, NY: SUNY Press.

Cunningham, A. F., & Parker, C. (1998, Summer). Tribal colleges as community institutions and resources. In J. P. Merisotis & C. T. O'Brien (Eds.), *New Directions for Higher Education: No. 102. Minority-serving institutions: Distinct purposes, common goals* (pp. 45–56). San Francisco, CA: Jossey-Bass.

Excelencia in Education. (2012/2013). *Emerging Hispanic-Serving Institutions (HSIs): 2012–2013* (Rep.). Retrieved from http://www.edexcelencia.org /research/2012-2013-hsi-lists

Gasman, M. (2013). *The changing face of historically Black colleges and universities.* Philadelphia: University of Pennsylvania, Center for MSIs.

Gasman, M., Baez, B., & Turner, C. (2008). *Understanding minority-serving institutions.* Albany: State University of New York Press.

Griffin, K. A., & Hurtado, S. (2011). Institutional variety in American higher education. In J. Schuh, S. Jones, & S. Harper (Eds.), *Student services: A handbook for the profession* (5th ed., pp. 24–42). San Francisco, CA: Jossey-Bass.

Guillory, J. P., & Ward, K. (2008). Tribal colleges and universities: Identity, invisibility and current issues. In M. Gasman, B. Baez, & C. Turner (Eds.), *Understanding minority-serving institutions* (pp. 91–110). Albany, NY: SUNY Press.

Harmon, N. (2012). *The role of minority-serving institutions in national college completion goals.* Washington, DC: Institute for Higher Education Policy.

Hispanic Association of Colleges and Universities. (2014). *About HACU.* Retrieved from http://www.hacu.net/hacu/HACU_101.asp?SnID=1850119513

Hurtado, S., Alvarez, C. L., Guillermo-Wann, C., Cuellar, M., & Arellano, L. (2012). A model for diverse learning environments: The scholarship on creating and assessing conditions for student success. In J. C. Smart & M. B. Paulsen (Eds.), *Higher education: Handbook of theory and research* (Vol. 27, pp. 41–122). New York, NY: Springer.

Kim, M. M., & Conrad, C. F. (2006). The impact of historical Black colleges and universities on the academic success of African-American students. *Research in Higher Education, 47*(4), 399–427.

Laden, B. V. (2004). Hispanic-Serving Institutions: What are they? Where are they? *Community College Journal of Research and Practice, 28*(3), 181–198.

Li, X. (2007). *Characteristics of minority-serving institutions and minority undergraduates enrolled in these institutions* (NCES 2008-156). Washington, DC: National Center for Education Statistics, Institute of Education Sciences, U.S. Department of Education.

Mercer, C. J., & Stedman, J. B. (2008). Minority-serving institutions: Selected institutional and student characteristics. In M. Gasman, B. Baez, & C. Turner (Eds.), *Understanding minority-serving institutions* (pp. 28–42). Albany, NY: SUNY Press.

Merisotis, J. P., & McCarthy, K. (2005). Retention and student success at minority-serving institutions. In G. H. Gaither (Ed.), *New Directions for Institutional Research: No. 125. What works: Achieving success in minority retention* (pp. 45–58). San Francisco, CA: Jossey-Bass.

National Commission on Asian American and Pacific Islander Research in Education. (2012). *Asian American and Native American Pacific Islander-Serving Institutions: Areas of growth, innovation, and collaboration.* Retrieved from http://care.gseis.ucla.edu/assets/care-brief-aanapisi_2012.pdf

Nunez, A. M., & Elizondo, D. (2012). *Hispanic-Serving Institutions in the US Mainland and Puerto Rico: Organizational characteristics, institutional financial context, and graduation outcomes.* A White Paper for HACU. Hispanic Association of Colleges and Universities.

O'Brien, E. M., & Zudak, C. (1998, Summer). Minority-serving institutions: An overview. In J. P. Merisotis & C. T. O'Brien (Eds.), *New Directions for Higher Education: No. 102. Minority-serving institutions: Distinct purposes, common goals* (pp. 5–15). San Francisco, CA: Jossey-Bass.

Palmer, R. T., Davis, R., & Hilton, A. (2009). Exploring challenges that threaten to impede the academic success of academically underprepared Black males at an HBCU. *Journal of College Student Development, 50*(4), 429–445.

Redd, K. E. (1998, Summer). Historically Black colleges and universities: Making a comeback. In J. P. Merisotis & C. T. O'Brien (Eds.), *New Directions in Higher Education: No. 102. Minority-serving institutions: Distinct purposes, common goals* (pp. 33–43). San Francisco, CA: Jossey-Bass.

Shotton, H. J., Lowe, S. C., & Waterman, S. J. (Eds.). (2013). *Beyond the asterisk: Understanding native students in higher education.* Sterling, VA: Stylus Publishing, LLC.

Southern Education Foundation. (2011). *The role of minority-serving institutions: In redefining and improving developmental education.* Atlanta, GA. Retrieved from http://www.southerneducation.org/cmspages/getfile.aspx?guid=45d0bedb-e6b0-45b5-98c8-02dc0815dbac

Stage, F. K., & Hubbard, S. M. (2009). Undergraduate institutions that foster women and minority scientists. *Journal of Women and Minorities in Science and Engineering, 15*, 77–91.

Stage, F. K., John, G., & Hubbard, S. (2011). Undergraduate institutions that foster Black scientists. In W. F. Tate & H. T. Frierson (Eds.), *Beyond stock stories and folktales: African Americans paths to STEM fields* (Vol. 11, pp. 3–21). Bingley, UK: Emerald Group Publishing.

Stage, F., Lundy-Wagner, V., & John, G. (2012). Minority-serving institutions and STEM: Charting the landscape. In R. Palmer, D. Maramba, & M. Gasman (Eds.), *Fostering success of ethnic and racial minorities in STEM: The role of minority-serving institutions* (pp. 16–32). New York, NY: Routledge.

Teranishi, R. T. (2012). Asian American and Pacific Islander students and the institutions that serve them. *Change: The Magazine of Higher Learning, 44*(2), 16–22.

U.S. Department of Education. (2012). *Asian American and Native American Pacific Islander-Serving Institutions program*. Retrieved from http://www2.ed.gov /about/inits/list/asian-americans-initiative/aanapisi.html

U.S. Department of Education. (2013). *Lists of postsecondary institutions enrolling populations with significant percentages of minority students*. Retrieved from http://www2.ed.gov/about/offices/list/ocr/edlite-minorityinst.html

U.S. Department of Education, National Center for Education Statistics (NCES). (2013a). *Integrated postsecondary education data survey*. Retrieved from http://nces.ed.gov/ipeds/

U.S. Department of Education, National Center for Education Statistics (NCES). (2013b, January). *Projections of education statistics to 2021* (Rep.). Retrieved from http://nces.ed.gov/pubs2013/2013008.pdf

U.S. Department of the Interior. (2013). *Minority-serving institutions program*. Retrieved from http://www.doi.gov/pmb/eeo/doi-minority-serving-institutions-program.cfm

The White House. (2013). *Higher education*. Retrieved from http://www.whitehouse .gov/issues/education/higher-education

GINELLE JOHN *is the enrollment administrator and an adjunct faculty instructor of research for the Department of Occupational Therapy at New York University.*

FRANCES K. STAGE *is a professor of higher and postsecondary education in the Department of Administration, Leadership, and Technology at New York University.*

NEW DIRECTIONS FOR INSTITUTIONAL RESEARCH • DOI: 10.1002/ir

Critical mixed methods approaches allow us to reflect upon the ways in which we collect, measure, interpret, and analyze data, providing novel alternatives for quantitative analysis. For institutional researchers, whose work influences institutional policies, programs, and practices, the approach has the transformative ability to expose and create space for altering rather than reproducing problematic institutional stratifications and inequities. The usefulness of this approach is illustrated here using examples from a critical mixed methods study of student pathways through postsecondary STEM education.

Disrupting the Pipeline: Critical Analyses of Student Pathways Through Postsecondary STEM Education

Heather E. Metcalf

Introduction and Purpose

In the 2011 State of the Union address, deemed "our generation's Sputnik moment," President Obama highlighted the role of science, technology, engineering, and mathematics (STEM) and STEM education in helping America "win the future" against the global competition (NPR, 2011). President Obama praised STEM innovation and clearly articulated the importance of educating American children so that they take on scientific jobs on behalf of the nation. A 2012 report by President Obama's Council of Advisors on Science and Technology issued a call for one million additional STEM college graduates be "produced" over the next decade so that nations that "out-educate us today will [not] out-compete us tomorrow" (PCAST, 2012, p. 7). This global competitiveness discourse views education as a means of producing large numbers of STEM workers and stretches back to the Cold War (Lucena, 2005; Metcalf, 2007, 2010, 2011).

In the 1970s, as lingering Cold War fears paired with emphasis on technological competition, the National Science Foundation developed the pipeline model underlying, though not named in, President Obama's speech and subsequent report. This model was used to quantify and predict the number of scientists and engineers necessary to fulfill national

NEW DIRECTIONS FOR INSTITUTIONAL RESEARCH, no. 158 © 2014 Wiley Periodicals, Inc.
Published online in Wiley Online Library (wileyonlinelibrary.com) • DOI: 10.1002/ir.20047

competitiveness needs by depicting a linear set of steps through various educational stages required to become a scientist or engineer as follows: "$Q_1 + \sum f_i - \sum f_o = Q_2$, Where Q_1 = the number of people in stock at the beginning of the period, $\sum f_i$ = the sum of flows into the stock, $\sum f_o$ = the sum of flows out of the stock, and Q_2 = the number of people in stock at the end of period" (Lucena, 2005, p. 105; National Research Council, 1986, p. 29). Those not "flowing" along the prescribed sequence are considered "leaks." Certain points are seen as particularly "leaky," especially for U.S. women and minorities.

This pipeline model has been the basis of recruitment and retention efforts aimed at women and people of color in STEM for the last 40 years and is expanding as a model for understanding education pathways more broadly, yet the problems of inequity, underrepresentation, and STEM workforce shortage are still proclaimed in the discourse of much current research and programming (Metcalf, 2007, 2010, 2011). This model has survived for decades despite critiques surrounding its flawed predictions and supply-side focus (Etzkowitz, Kemelgor, & Uzzi, 2000; Lucena, 2005; Teitelbaum, 2003), poor measurements (Lucena, 2005), linearity and inability to account for varied career paths (Xie & Shauman, 2003), tendency to homogenize people, fields, sectors, and stages, discursive view of people as passive pipeline "flow," and lack of focus on systemic change and power relations, particularly those related to gender, race, class, sexuality, ability, and citizenship (Hammonds & Subramaniam, 2003; Husu, 2001).

The flaws of the pipeline metaphor have become embedded, in various ways, as assumptions within the majority of STEM workforce studies and the surveys and data sets upon which they are based. Consequently, its use for understanding and measuring STEM educational and career paths and expansion as a model for education in general is particularly problematic. Solutions to the leaky pipeline focus on patching the leaks and/or increasing the input and hoping for more output, oversimplifying what constitutes participation in STEM, and leaving the pipes themselves unchanged.

This chapter seeks to illustrate how a critical mixed methods approach can allow us to understand how the pipeline model ideology has become embedded within academic discourse, research, and data surrounding STEM education and work and to provide novel alternatives for quantitative analysis. Here, I first discuss the usefulness of critical theoretical frameworks and how these can be applied to quantitative analyses. Then, I illustrate how I applied this approach to my own research on the STEM workforce by offering examples from my critical analysis of the workforce data and subsequent logistic regression analyses of that data (see Metcalf [2011] for the full analysis).

Theoretical Framework

The theoretical bases of this project come from critical theory. Originating in the 1920s critical theory builds on Marxist critiques of capitalism to offer broader social and cultural critiques (Habermas, 1971). Critical theory is "self-conscious, self-critical and non-objectifying" (Macey, 2000, p. 75) and aims to reveal "hidden power arrangements, oppressive practices, and ways of thinking... for the purpose of changing society to make it more just" (Baez, 2007, p. 19). Critical theory encourages reading through ideology for hidden subtexts, omissions, and answers to questions unposed in order to disrupt, destabilize, and denaturalize those ideologies. Viewing the pipeline model through the lens of ideology attends to its discursive and material existence and provides a way to see through the illusion to the underlying power dynamics and oppressive beliefs allowing for its reproduction.

Critical theory stems from a history of emancipatory and social-transformative goals and is particularly attentive to language, knowledge production, power, oppression, and their reproduction. Critical theorists often see the relationship between concepts (e.g., gender) and subjects (e.g., people) as unstable, fluid, and historically, socially, and politically mediated (Baez, 2007; Soto, 2005). Contemporary critical theory argues for the importance of considering the inseparable and complex intricacies, histories, and contexts among identities, particularly those that have traditionally been theorized and researched individually (Baez, 2007; Crenshaw, 1991).

Applying critical theoretical lenses to science as a social and cultural text, feminist science studies have greatly informed this project. The feminism in feminist science studies is not just about the study of women or gender, but involves the broader study of entangled and inseparable systems of power, oppression, and subject formation. Such scholars have considered the history of hierarchy, oppression, and exclusion within science and engineering (Hacker, 1989; Oldenziel, 2004; Tobias, 1993). This work raises questions about bias and knowledge construction in science and engineering scholarship (Fausto-Sterling, 2000; Martin, 1998), problematizes the very notion of objectivity, interrogates the gendered, classed, sexualized, and racialized assumptions underlying such work, and questions the overall project of "science" and positivism (Haraway, 1991; Harding, 2006; Keller, 2001). This scholarship has illustrated how STEM work has been and is connected to militarism, environmental destruction, global capitalism, research used against or to "prove" the inferiority of women and people of color, and "the failure of the transfer of Western sciences and technologies to the developing world to benefit the vast majority of the globe's least-advantaged citizens" (Harding, 2006, pp. 4–5). This work charged me to think critically about scientific claims and claims about science and identity in workforce and pipeline studies and to question the assumptions made therein. While many critical theorists utilize qualitative methodologies in their work, they have also demonstrated that, despite problematic aspects of our scientific and quantitative histories, it is possible and necessary to conduct scientific and quantitative work from critical and socially just perspectives.

NEW DIRECTIONS FOR INSTITUTIONAL RESEARCH • DOI: 10.1002/ir

Methodology

Within higher education, there is a growing interest in critical quantitative analysis (e.g., Baez, 2007; Browne, 2007; Carter & Hurtado, 2007; Kinzie, 2007; Stage, 2007). Baez (2007) explains that this kind of analysis asks how research "can be critically transformative—that is, to what extent educational research can offer critiques of our world that allow us to transform it" (p. 18). He further elaborates that "the idea of critical must be understood in particular contexts, and such an understanding has to recognize the politics and political arrangements associated with such an idea" (p. 19). He argues that critical theory, critical reflection of self, attentiveness to how research and the institutions in which it is conducted are implicated in oppression, and a focus on transformative outcomes form the nexus of critical quantitative research.

Critical quantitative research takes into deep consideration the variables and their underlying measures, contexts (social, political, historical, etc.), and potential interpretations and the implications of each of these for respondents, researchers, policy makers, communities, etc. For example, critical theory allows us to look more deeply at survey design and its role in the construction of "proper subjects" (Althusser, 1971). Surveys, particularly digital surveys, lay the foundation for proper subjects by detailing the categories with which a respondent may freely select to identify. These categories "hail" individuals as subjects in very particular and power-laden ways. For example, the first question on many demographic sections of surveys asks for a participant's "gender," with the "acceptable" categories of response most often being male or female. Participants who answer the call enter into a performance of marking a checkbox indicating that they acquiesce to the dominant ideology that their gender can be represented by these fixed, binary, and biologically based categories. Those who do not answer the call mark themselves as "bad" subjects and, in the digital case, as nonsubjects who may not proceed with the survey. They are rendered marginal, other, and even "abject" despite many lived experiences of gender as fluid (Butler, 1999; Spivak, 1988). Critical theory, then, allows for an analysis that looks between the lines of surveys and existing data to see who and what counts as the proper subjects of STEM and to suggest new possibilities for understanding the "real" experiences of those who do not necessarily fit into the ideological illusion.

Critical quantitative research allows us to see and acknowledge the limitations in our data sets, construct new measures, *and* find ways to engage with and contextualize the data, despite these limitations, in critical ways. This chapter applies a critical theoretical approach to reading the 2006 SESTAT surveys and data, with a focus on how STEM participation and demographic identities are measured, and illustrates new ways of thinking about what counts as STEM work and who counts as a STEM participant through examples from my critical logistic regression analyses of the data.

New Directions for Institutional Research • DOI: 10.1002/ir

Data, Sample, and Measures

As discussed in my previous work (Metcalf, 2010, 2011), the nationally representative data set most often used in studies of the STEM workforce is the National Science Foundation's Scientists and Engineers Statistical Data System (SESTAT) data. The target population for SESTAT is U.S. residents who have at least a bachelor's degree by June 30 of the previous year and who, during the survey reference period, were noninstitutionalized, 75 years of age or younger, and either educated in a science and engineering field or working in a science and engineering occupation. The SESTAT data come from three national-level surveys—the National Survey of College Graduates, the National Survey of Recent College Graduates, and the Survey of Doctorate Recipients—each of which collects information on respondents' employment, education, and demographics. The surveys are compiled into a single comprehensive database with new data added every two to three years since 1993 (National Science Foundation, 2008). The most recent data available at the time of this analysis were collected in 2006 ($n = 105,064$).

STEM Measures.   Embedded in these surveys are the NSF's categories for what counts as science and engineering and what does not. The NSF defines scientists and engineers as those who either received a college degree (bachelor's or higher) in a science or engineering field or who work as a scientist or engineer and have a bachelor's degree or higher in any field (National Science Foundation, 2008), automatically discounting those who might do scientific or engineering work without a formal education or who received an associate's degree. While the individual surveys that are compiled to construct the SESTAT database ask questions about community college attendance and associate's degrees, these data are only occasionally included in the SESTAT integrated database, largely because the target population for the database is those who have at least a bachelor's degree (National Science Foundation, 2008, 2009). This limits the potential to understand STEM educational pathways for those with community college experiences.

The NSF also defines science and engineering fields and degrees through the use of six categories: computer and mathematical sciences; biological, agricultural, and other life sciences;[1] physical and related sciences;[2] social and related sciences;[3] engineering; and teaching in any of these areas at a postsecondary level, which is also included as science and engineering (S&E) work. However, the degrees and occupations listed in Table 7.1 do not count. Notably, a computer science degree counts, yet a programming occupation does not. Likewise, teaching science and engineering in a higher education setting counts, but at a K–12 level it does not. Technology degrees also do not count, despite the ways in which science and technology are frequently paired.

Given the trend in higher education for academic capitalist modes of knowledge production which encourage partnerships among faculty, managerial professionals, and workers in industry across a variety of

New Directions for Institutional Research • DOI: 10.1002/ir

Table 7.1. Non-science and Engineering Degrees and Occupations

Non-science and Engineering Degrees	Non-science and Engineering Occupations
Business administration, business and managerial economics	Managers and administrators
Health fields, bachelor's and master's level	Health-related occupations (doctors and other health practitioners, nurses, pharmacists, therapists, health technologists, and technicians)
Education fields	Precollege teachers; postsecondary teachers in non-S&E fields
Social services and related fields (social work, philosophy, religion, and theology)	Social services occupations (clergy, counselors and social workers)
Technologies fields (computer programming, data processing, and engineering)	Technologists and technicians (computer programmers and technicians in S&E fields)
Sales and market fields	Sales and marketing occupations
Art and humanities fields	Artists and other humanities occupations (artists, editors, writers, and non-S&T historians)

Source: National Science Foundation (2008).

different fields, there is increasing boundary blurring between the private and public sectors as well as between disciplines (Harding, 2006; Slaughter & Rhoades, 2004). As academic capitalism provides the most benefits to fields that are closest to the market (most often those which involve science and technology), numerous non-technology-based fields are building relationships with those that are technology based. Biotechnology is a prime example of this, but certainly not the only one. Graphic design in art departments, educational technology in education departments, entrepreneurial science courses, technology transfer management, and science patenting law are other examples of this blending. One might expect more fields to involve technology, scientific work to have elements of the "non-sciences," and the "non-sciences" to incorporate scientific work. As Etzkowitz et al. (2000) point out, "[a]lthough not unemployed, young physicists can often be found utilizing their quantitative and analytical skills in the back rooms of Wall Street or even in their own financial firms" (p. 2). These partnerships and blurred boundaries are not represented in these definitions of science and engineering/non-science and engineering, reducing the accuracy with which researchers can understand what constitutes scientific work.

Identity Measures. Another large and limiting bias in the SESTAT surveys and the studies based off of them is that its gender and racial identity measures are biologically based. These surveys measure gender using a dichotomous male/female variable and race with a set of mutually exclusive categories. A considerable amount of work has been done within women's studies, gender studies, and feminist science studies to refute this dichotomy. Even if gender, which is fluid, socially constructed, historically contextual, and highly performative, were the same as biological sex, intersex as a category of biological sex is excluded as a survey response option (Butler, 1999; Fausto-Sterling, 2000; Kessler, 2001).

Race and ethnicity, also fluid, performative, and socially constructed (Omi & Winant, 1994) are often merged together and the use of mutually exclusive and limited categories does not allow respondents to indicate various mixed racial identifications. Following the United States Census categories, each of the 2006 SESTAT surveys asks respondents if they are Hispanic or Latino as a measure of ethnicity and then provides four mutually exclusive subcategories for those who answer in the affirmative: Mexican or Chicano, Puerto Rican, Cuban, or other. Then, all respondents are asked to mark one or more of the following racial categories: American Indian or Alaska Native, Native Hawaiian or other Pacific Islander, Asian, Black or African American, or White. While the racial options on the surveys allow for multicategory identification, the Latino/a ethnicity questions do not. Additionally, other racial and ethnic subcommunities are left unrepresented on the surveys. For example, Chinese, Filipino, Indian, Vietnamese, Korean, and Japanese (among others) communities are wrapped up and homogenized in the Asian category despite that critical race research has shown drastically different social and educational experiences between those who identify with these groups (Teranishi, 2002).

Race and ethnicity responses are then compiled in the SESTAT database into a number of variables including indicator variables for each of the racial categories and for the broad Hispanic or Latino ethnicity category and a "minority" indicator variable for all respondents who indicated that their race or ethnicity was anything but White or Asian. The responses are also used to create two additional race/ethnicity variables within SESTAT that, along with the "minority" indicator, are most often used by researchers. The first race/ethnicity variable uses the Hispanic/Latino indicator as its own category and groups all racial categories together within it under the label "Hispanic, any race." It then distinguishes each of the racial categories separately from that indicator with the following categories: Asian, non-Hispanic only; American Indian or Alaska Native, non-Hispanic only; Native Hawaiian or other Pacific Islander, non-Hispanic only; Black or African American, non-Hispanic only; White, non-Hispanic only; Multiracial, non-Hispanic; or Hispanic, any race. This construct does not allow for an analysis of those who identify as multiracial (or any other race for that matter) and Hispanic. The second race/ethnicity variable rolls the Hispanic/Latino indicator into each of the racial categories so that there is no separate Hispanic classification as follows: Asian, American Indian or Alaska Native, Native Hawaiian or other Pacific Islander, Black or African American, White, or Multiracial. Asian, for example, now represents those who marked Asian and no other racial category but who also may or may not have indicated that they are of Hispanic/Latino ethnicity. This construct does not allow for an analysis that disaggregates among Hispanic/Latino and non-Hispanic/Latino identities. Additionally, the surveys do not allow individuals to identify as Hispanic/Latino only. Respondents have to select at least one racial category in addition to Hispanic or Latino ethnicity, and, if they chose to leave the question completely blank, a response was imputed for them using imputation classes and donor records (National Science Foundation, 2010). While researchers could use the series of indicator variables to create their own constructs, these prefabricated variables encourage otherwise and point both to the contextual underpinnings of racial and ethnic definitions and the highly subjective choices that are made in quantitative studies.

Not all of the assumptions in studies using the SESTAT data can be credited to survey construction. Most studies that consider gender and race look at these identity factors separately, comparing males in the aggregate to females in the aggregate (e.g., Abriola & Davies, 2006; Rapoport, 2004) and Whites to various racial groups, sometimes disaggregated to a limited extent and at other times aggregated to a "minority" group (e.g., Castillo-Chavez & Castillo-Garsow, 2006). Regardless of motivation, the pipeline model and many of these studies have as an end goal the recruitment and retention of historically underrepresented groups. Although this is an important aim, such a limited understanding of identity not only marginalizes those who do not see themselves reflected in the data collection instruments but also restricts the understanding researchers could have of the STEM workforce.

In the regression analysis examples that I provide below, I compare and contrast a number of ways of constructing identity measures, despite the survey limitations, to illustrate the degree to which our understanding of who is retained in STEM can shift based on our ways of measuring "who." Many studies and policy initiatives rely on statistical significance over exploring the experiences of the very populations they are purporting to attempt to recruit and retain. Statistical significance in and of itself is not reason enough to exclude particular groups from analysis, as is often the case for studies that exclude, for example, Native American respondents from their samples.[4] In many cases, the smaller number of respondents results in lower levels of significance despite very meaningful and interesting patterns that should not be overlooked.

Just as failing to have a respondent's identity represented on a survey in the first place can render them as abject or a nonsubject, disregarding these populations in the cutting, slicing, and grouping of data can result in a powerful systematic erasure of the experiences of already marginalized groups. This work highlights the importance of considering between and within group patterns and exploring varying levels of disaggregation of racial and ethnic categories in the study of retention. By not focusing solely on statistical significance in this work, I have opted to return to the questions of whether, why, and what retention patterns are occurring, even for smaller subgroups of respondents. The implications of the resulting findings are that researchers, practitioners, and even policy makers can begin to gain insights into groups often excluded by narrow statistical significance foci.

Retention Measures.   Pipeline discourse often argues for workforce shortages as a rationale for increasing STEM supply (Metcalf, 2010, 2011), yet very little quantitative research has considered the connection between supply and demand. As such, here I focus on different ways of thinking about and contextualizing retention between degree attainment and workforce entry. Much of the higher education research on retention focuses on retention and persistence as bachelor's degree attainment. These studies use measures such as academic and social involvement, adjustment, and integration, high school and college grade point average, college goal commitments, course enrollment, and social, cultural, and economic capital (Eitle & Eitle, 2002; Perna & Titus, 2005; Seidman, 2007). In particular, higher education research on major choice, access, and persistence in STEM have included predictors such as achievement, aptitude (as measured by SAT scores), attitudes toward STEM, course-taking patterns, and institution type, size, and selectivity, as well as other factors like self-concept, beliefs about mathematics, STEM behaviors, student values, social and cultural capital, and stereotype threat (Dowd, Malcom, & Macias, 2010; Kinzie, 2007; Seymour, 2001).

However, these studies all focus on persistence in terms of degree attainment in a STEM major and do not look at what students do with their degrees upon graduation. Instead, they tend to look at transitions that occur between K–12 and higher education, including a look at community college transfers. Little research has been done to consider if any of these factors predict or are associated with continuation in the same or a related field upon graduating. Part, but not all, of this has to do with the type of information collected in the national-level surveys. Because my work has a particular focus on the connection between supply, demand, and identity within retention discourse and because of limitations within the SESTAT data, many of these traditional measures are not used in this study. Instead, I focused on the influence of key demographic measures at varying levels of disaggregation on several retention-related outcomes as a way to compare alternative models to the traditional pipeline model.

Dependent Variables: Alternative Measures for Retention Into the Workforce

Key-dependent variables selected from the 2006 SESTAT data were based on my analyses of the workforce studies, surveys, and data and are used to measure various aspects of retention as an outcome (Metcalf, 2011). First, to represent the traditional pipeline discourse, I constructed a dichotomous pipeline "leak" variable as a measure of retention during respondents' transitions between obtaining their highest degrees and entering into the workforce postdegree. In accordance with the discourse, respondents are considered to be "leaks" if they obtained their highest degree in a field defined as S&E by the NSF but then went on to employment in a field defined as non-S&E by the NSF.

Second, the level of relatedness between respondents' highest degrees and their current occupations was used as an alternative measure of retention and ordered dependent variable. This variable resulted from a subjective survey question that asked the respondents to select among the following how related their highest degrees and occupations are: not related, somewhat related, or closely related.

Independent Variables

Based on the critical discourse analysis of the STEM workforce studies, surveys, and data, key independent variables were selected for analysis from the 2006 SESTAT data, including identity/demographic variables (sex, race/ethnicity, citizenship, family, physical disabilities, age, salary, and parental education), employment-related variables (employment status, field, and sector), and education-related variables (degree type, field, and year) and were used with varying levels of disaggregation depending on the model (Metcalf, 2010, 2011). While limited by the SESTAT surveys in how they can account for the complexity of identity and experience, these variables still offer many possibilities for retention-related analyses. Since the discussion of these regression analyses is intended to illustrate the usefulness of critical quantitative perspectives, I limit the discussion that follows to examining the findings surrounding sex and race/ethnicity.[5]

Regression Analyses and Findings

Because the pipeline narrative is concerned about predicting STEM workforce needs and shortages, particularly surrounding women and minorities, the method of analysis selected must also be able to model the relationship between identity factors and STEM participation in a predictive fashion. As such, I used a series of logistic regressions to replicate and then challenge the pipeline discourse.

Binary Logistic Regression Models. First, I conducted three binary logistic regressions using pipeline "leaks" as the dependent retention variable. For the first regression, I followed the traditional pipeline model assumptions that tend to oversimplify identity characteristics by focusing dichotomously and mutually exclusively on women and minorities. The second binary logistic model disaggregated identity characteristics where possible. To further complicate identity measures and consider the experiences of, for example, women of color, the third model is a full interaction

Table 7.2. Binary Logistic Regression-Dependent Variable: Highest Degree/Occupation Leak

Explanatory Variables	(1) Traditional Pipeline Exp(B)	(2) Disaggregated Model Exp(B)	(3) Interaction Model— Males Exp(B)	(4) Interaction Model— Females Exp(B)
Female	1.377*	1.41*	–	–
Minority	1.280*	–	–	–
American Indian/Alaska Native, non-Hispanic only[a]	–	1.201	1.188	1.242
Asian, non-Hispanic only[a]	–	0.883*	0.896**	0.902***
Black, non-Hispanic only[a]	–	1.525*	1.705*	1.389*
Native Hawaiian/Pacific Islander, non-Hispanic only[a]	–	0.932	1.315*	1.291*
Hispanic, any race[a]	–	1.304*	1.144	0.694
Multiracial, non-Hispanic only[a]	–	1.176***	1.133	1.195

Notes: Odds ratio terms are reported and an intercept term is included in each model. *, **, and *** indicate statistically significant at the .001, .01, and .05 levels, respectively. $n = 105,064$.
[a] Race/ethnicity categories presented are in comparison to the category "White, non-Hispanic only."

binary logistic regression model that interacted the sex variable with each of the independent variables that were included in the second model. This model, shown as one model for males and one for females in Table 7.2, was intended to represent the complicated ways in which sex as a social construct overlaps and is intertwined with other identity and social factors.

Findings.   As Table 7.2, model 1 shows, the traditional pipeline model had the expected results: when holding all other variables constant, females, and racial and ethnic minorities were found to have higher odds of "leaking" between obtaining their highest degrees and occupations than their respective counterparts.

However, by disaggregating various measures for race/ethnicity and interacting sex and race/ethnicity variables, we find that retention resists the simple "women and minorities are leaking" story often espoused by the traditional pipeline narrative. Models 2–4 in Table 7.2 show that not all racial/ethnic minority groups have equal likelihoods of "leaking." Though not statistically significant, while holding all other predictors constant, model 2 shows that non-Hispanic Native Hawaiian/Pacific Islanders have slightly lower odds of being highest degree to occupation leaks than those who are White, non-Hispanic and slightly higher odds of leaking than those who are Asian, non-Hispanic. Those who are Asian, non-Hispanic have odds of leaking that are nearly 15% less than those who are White, non-Hispanic. Black, non-Hispanic respondents have the highest odds of leaking and have odds of leaking that are about seven times higher than American Indian/Alaska Natives with similar findings when comparing American Indian/Alaska Natives to those who are Hispanic or multiracial.

Further complicating this picture, models 3 and 4 in Table 7.2 show the key findings from the full interaction model. Holding all other variables constant, for both females and males, identifying as non-Hispanic American Indian/Alaska Native, non-Hispanic Black, non-Hispanic Native Hawaiian/Pacific Islander, or non-Hispanic multiracial is associated with greater odds of leaking than it is for White, non-Hispanic, or Asian, non-Hispanic females and males, respectively. In a particularly notable difference, however, for males, identifying as Black or Hispanic has a larger impact on a respondent's odds of leaking than it does for females, and for females, identifying as non-Hispanic American Indian/Alaska Native or multiracial has a larger impact on a respondent's odds of leaking than it does for males. These findings demonstrate that accounting for race and ethnicity in retention, even when measured as pipeline leaks, is not as simple as minority versus nonminority.

The deeper levels of disaggregation used in the models 2, 3, and 4 demonstrate two major points: first, there is great variation in retention likelihood within and between racial and ethnic minority groups, particularly when mediated by sex, that is largely unaccounted for in the pipeline ideology; second, contrary to much contemporary discourse, it is both possible and feasible to construct models that better account for some of the complexity surrounding identity that the traditional pipeline washes over, even when retention is conceptualized narrowly as pipeline "leaks."

Ordered Logistic Regression Models.   For the final regression models, I used ordered logistic regression to consider highest degree-occupation relatedness as an alternative to leaking as measure of retention outcomes for those who were employed at the time of the survey. Degree-occupation relatedness is a measure of respondents' perceptions of how closely related their degrees are to their current occupations. This measure of retention accounts for perceived use of one's degree in their day-to-day work. As in the binary logistic models, I first modeled the pipeline assumptions about how to account for identity via a basic set of indicator independent variables. Then, I expanded the model to account for disaggregated identity characteristics.

Findings.   Model 1 in Table 7.3 represents the basic pipeline identity assumptions and shows that, holding the other predictors constant, females are more likely than males and minorities are less likely than nonminorities to have high degree-occupation relatedness. While the pipeline model in Table 7.2 showed that females are *less* likely to be retained than males, with a different conceptualization of retention, model 1 in Table 7.3 shows that females are *more* likely than males to be retained.

Similarly, the expanded models also illustrate that it is possible for individuals to be likely to leak yet also likely to have close connections between their STEM degrees and occupations and vice versa. While model 2,

Table 7.3. Ordered Logistic Regression-Dependent Variable: Degree-Occupation Relatedness

Explanatory Variables	(1) Basic Pipeline Identity Measures Exp(B)	(2) Expanded Identity Measures Exp(B)
Sex	1.032***	0.973
Minority	0.953**	–
American Indian/Alaska Native, non-Hispanic only[a]	–	1.206***
Asian, non-Hispanic only[a]	–	0.903*
Black, non-Hispanic only[a]	–	0.938***
Native Hawaiian/Pacific Islander, non-Hispanic only[a]	–	0.856
Hispanic, any race[a]	–	1.04
Multiracial, non-Hispanic only[a]	–	0.804*

Notes: For models 1 and 2, odds ratio terms are reported and an intercept term is included in each model. *, **, and *** indicate statistically significant at the .001, .01, and .05 levels, respectively. n = 90,711.
[a]Race/ethnicity categories presented are in comparison to the category "White, non-Hispanic only."

Table 7.2 showed that non-Hispanic American Indian/Native Alaskans and Hispanics of any race have greater likelihoods of leaking than White, non-Hispanics, model 2, Table 7.3 shows that these groups also have greater likelihoods than White non-Hispanics of having high degree-occupation relatedness. While model 2, Table 7.2 shows that non-Hispanic Native Hawaiian/Pacific Islanders have odds of leaking that are about 10% less than White non-Hispanics, model 2, Table 7.3 shows that non-Hispanic Native Hawaiian/Pacific Islanders have odds that are about 14% less than White non-Hispanics of having high degree-occupation relatedness. In many cases, those who were least likely to be retained according to the pipeline models were the *most* likely to be retained in the degree-occupation relatedness models (e.g., females, and minorities, especially non-Hispanic American Indian/Native Alaskans and Hispanics).

Significance and Conclusion

Considerable research, policy, and programmatic efforts have been dedicated to addressing the participation of particular populations in STEM for decades. These efforts include but are certainly not limited to the creation of journals, policy-induced task forces, legal acts, massive research and program grants, national organizations, and institutional organizations. Each of these efforts claims equity-related goals, yet, they often heavily frame the problem, through pipeline discourse, in terms of national needs, workforce supply, and competitiveness. This particular framing of the problem may, indeed, be counter to equity goals, especially when paired with policy

NEW DIRECTIONS FOR INSTITUTIONAL RESEARCH • DOI: 10.1002/ir

that largely relies on statistical significance and broad aggregation of data over exploring the identities and experiences of the populations targeted for equitable outcomes in that policy. Without deeper understandings of the experiences of these targeted populations and without a focus on change that extends beyond the individual to address the many systemic and institutional issues described here, little progress toward realizing equity goals can be expected (Etzkowitz et al., 2000).

Regardless of intention, many workforce studies and their underlying data sets have a tendency to greatly oversimplify the ways in which retention outcomes and rationales, especially for targeted underrepresented groups, are measured and understood. Applying a critical eye to how retention and identity are conceptualized, regardless of whether the mode of analysis falls into qualitative and/or quantitative camps, is just one step toward deepening our understanding of retention issues. Increasing the depth and breadth of our understanding in turn helps generate a richer pool of resources to aid interested parties in achieving, rather than undermining, their ultimate equity-based goals.

Many subjective choices are made in the construction of large-scale data sets used to inform much national science and engineering policy and these choices greatly influence the likelihood of retention outcomes. What counts as science and engineering, and who counts as a scientist and engineer, is socially constructed. Despite these limitations in existing data, with a critical lens, we can still do much to analyze the data in novel ways that may better allow for the complexities of experiences and identities to be reflected.

This chapter highlights the importance and usefulness of critically looking at the ways in which we collect, measure, interpret, and analyze data. For institutional researchers, whose work influences institutional policies, programs, and practice, such an approach has the transformative ability to expose and create space for altering rather than reproducing problematic institutional arrangements, stratifications, and inequities. By calling into question our own and others' underlying assumptions, methods, models, and measures, broadening our thinking, and richly contextualizing our work, we step outside our comfort zones to open up the possibility of seeing our institutions and our worlds differently and changing them.

Notes

1. These include agricultural, food, biological, medical, and environmental life sciences as well as health sciences at the doctoral level.
2. These include chemistry, earth science, geology, oceanography, physics, and astronomy.
3. These include economics, political science, psychology, sociology, anthropology, and science and technology history.
4. In their book, *The Cult of Statistical Significance: How the Standard Error Costs Us Job, Justice, and Lives*, Ziliak and McCloskey (2011) argue, "for the past eighty years it

appears that some of the sciences have made a mistake by basing decisions on statistical 'significance'...which should be a tiny part of an inquiry concerned with the size and importance of relationships" (pp. 2–3). They explain that focus on statistical significance has come at the expense of broader philosophical inquiry such that, instead of asking whether or why certain phenomena are occurring, researchers have begun instead focusing on how much of the phenomena are occurring.

5. For the full models and resulting findings, please see Metcalf (2011).

References

Abriola, L. M., & Davies, M. W. (2006). Attracting and retaining women in engineering: The Tufts experience. In *CHERI Policy Research Conference: Doctoral Education and the Faculty of the Future*. Retrieved from http://www.ilr.cornell.edu/cheri/conferences/upload/2006/Abriola.pdf

Althusser, L. (1971). Ideology and ideological state apparatuses: Notes toward an investigation. In B. Brewster (Ed. & Trans.), *Lenin and philosophy and other essays* (pp. 127–184). New York, NY: Monthly Review Press.

Baez, B. (2007). Thinking critically about the "critical": Quantitative research as social critique. In F. K. Stage (Ed.), *New Directions for Institutional Research: No. 133. Using quantitative data to answer critical questions* (pp. 17–23). San Francisco, CA: Jossey-Bass.

Browne, K. (2007). Selling my queer soul or queerying quantitative research. *Sociological Research Online*, 13(1). Retrieved from http://www.socresonline.org.uk/13/1/11.html

Butler, J. (1999). *Gender trouble: Feminism and the subversion of identity* (2nd ed.). New York, NY: Routledge.

Carter, D. F., & Hurtado, S. (2007). Quantitative research using a critical eye. In F. K. Stage (Ed.), *New Directions for Institutional Research: No. 133. Using quantitative data to answer critical questions* (pp. 25–35). San Francisco, CA: Jossey-Bass.

Castillo-Chavez, C., & Castillo-Garsow, C. (2006). Increasing minority representation in the mathematical sciences: Good models but no will to scale up their impact. In *CHERI Conference: Doctoral Education and the Faculty of the Future*. Retrieved from http://www.ilr.cornell.edu/cheri/conferences/upload/2006/Castillo-Chavez.pdf

Crenshaw, K. (1991). Mapping the margins: Intersectionality, identity politics, and violence against women of color. *Stanford Law Review*, 43(6), 1241–1299.

Dowd, A. C., Malcom, L. E., & Macias, E. E. (2010). *Improving transfer access to STEM bachelor's degrees at Hispanic-Serving Institutions through the America COMPETES act*. Los Angeles: University of Southern California.

Eitle, T., & Eitle, D. (2002). Race, cultural capital, and the educational effects of participation in sports. *Sociology of Education*, 75, 123–146.

Etzkowitz, H., Kemelgor, C., & Uzzi, B. (2000). *Athena unbound: The advancement of women in science and technology*. Cambridge, UK: Cambridge University Press.

Fausto-Sterling, A. (2000). *Sexing the body: Gender politics and the construction of sexuality*. New York, NY: Basic Books.

Habermas, J. (1971). *Knowledge and human interests: Theory and practice, communication, and the evolution of society* (J. Shapiro, Trans.). London, UK: Heinemann.

Hacker, S. (1989). *Power, pleasure, and technology: Some tales of gender, engineering, and the cooperative workplace*. Boston, MA: Unwin Hyman.

Hammonds, E., & Subramaniam, B. (2003). A conversation on feminist science studies. *Signs: Journal of Women in Culture and Society*, 28(3), 923–944.

Haraway, D. (1991). Situated knowledges: The science question in feminism and the privilege of partial perspective. In *Simians, cyborgs, and women: The reinvention of nature* (pp. 183–203). New York, NY: Routledge.

Harding, S. (2006). *Science and social inequality: Feminist and postcolonial issues.* Urbana: University of Illinois Press.

Husu, L. (2001). On metaphors on the position of women in academia and science. *NORA, 9*(3), 172–181.

Keller, E. F. (2001). From working scientist to feminist critic. In M. Lederman & I. Bartsch (Eds.), *The gender and science reader* (pp. 59–62). New York, NY: Routledge.

Kessler, S. (2001). The medical construction of gender: Case management of intersexed infants. In M. Wyer et al. (Eds.), *Women, science, and technology: A reader in feminist science studies* (pp. 161–174). New York, NY: Routledge.

Kinzie, J. (2007). Women's paths in science: A critical feminist analysis. In F. K. Stage (Ed.), *New Directions for Institutional Research: No. 133. Using quantitative data to answer critical questions* (pp. 81–93). San Francisco, CA: Jossey-Bass.

Lucena, J. (2005). *Defending the nation: U.S. policymaking to create scientists and engineers from Sputnik to the "war against terrorism."* Boulder, CO: University Press of America.

Macey, D. (2000). *Dictionary of critical theory.* New York, NY: Penguin Books.

Martin, E. (1998). Anthropology and the cultural study of science. *Science, Technology, & Human Values, 23*(1), 24–44.

Metcalf, H. (2007). *Recruitment, retention, and diversity discourse: Problematizing the "problem" of women and minorities in science and engineering* (Master's thesis). University of Arizona, Tucson, AZ.

Metcalf, H. (2010). Stuck in the pipeline: A critical review of STEM workforce literature. *Interactions: UCLA Journal of Education and Information Studies, 6*(2), article 4.

Metcalf, H. (2011). *Formation and representation: Critical analyses of identity, supply, and demand in science, technology, engineering, and mathematics* (Doctoral dissertation). University of Arizona, Tucson, AZ.

National Research Council. (1986). *Engineering infrastructure diagramming and modeling.* Washington, DC: National Academies Press.

National Science Foundation. (2008). *Scientists and engineers statistical data system (SESTAT).* Retrieved from http://www.nsf.gov/statistics/sestat/sestatfaq.cfm

National Science Foundation. (2009). *SESTAT degree inventory.* Retrieved from http://sestat.nsf.gov/docs/inventory.html

National Science Foundation. (2010). *SESTAT survey design and methodology: Missing data imputation.* Retrieved from http://www.nsf.gov/statistics/sestat/missingdata.cfm

NPR. (2011). *Transcript: Obama's state of the union address.* Retrieved from http://www.npr.org/2011/01/26/133224933/transcript-obamas-state-of-union-address

Oldenziel, R. (2004). *Making technology masculine: Men, women, and modern machines in America, 1870–1945.* Amsterdam, The Netherlands: Amsterdam University Press.

Omi, M., & Winant, H. (1994). *Racial formation in the United States: From the 1960s to the 1980s.* New York, NY: Routledge.

PCAST. (2012). *Engage to excel: Producing one million additional college graduates with degrees in science, technology, engineering, and mathematics.* Retrieved from http://www.whitehouse.gov/sites/default/files/microsites/ostp/pcast-engage-to-excel-final_2-25-12.pdf

Perna, L., & Titus, M. (2005). The relationship between parental involvement as social capital and college enrollment: An examination of racial/ethnic group differences. *The Journal of Higher Education, 76*(5), 485–518.

Rapoport, A. (2004). *Gender differences in the careers of academic scientists and engineers.* Arlington, VA: National Science Foundation. Retrieved from http://www.nsf.gov/statistics/nsf04323/front.htm

Seidman, A. (Ed.). (2007). *Minority student retention: The best of the journal of college student retention: Research, theory & practice.* Amityville, NY: Baywood Publishing Company.

Seymour, E. (2001). Tracking the processes of change in U.S. undergraduate education in science, mathematics, engineering, and technology. *Science Education, 86*(1), 79–105.

Slaughter, S., & Rhoades, G. (2004). *Academic capitalism and the new economy markets, state, and higher education.* Baltimore, MD: Johns Hopkins University Press.

Soto, S. (2005). Cherríe Moraga's going brown: "Reading like a queer." *GLQ: A Journal of Lesbian and Gay Studies, 11*(2), 237–263.

Spivak, G. C. (1988). Can the subaltern speak? In C. Nelson & L. Grossberg (Eds.), *Marxism and the interpretation of culture* (pp. 271–313). Urbana: University of Illinois Press.

Stage, F. K. (2007). Answering critical questions using quantitative data. In F. K. Stage (Ed.), *New Directions for Institutional Research: No. 133. Using quantitative data to answer critical questions* (pp. 5–16). San Francisco, CA: Jossey-Bass.

Teitelbaum, M. S. (2003). Do we need more scientists? *Public Interest, 153,* 40–53.

Teranishi, R. (2002). Asian Pacific Americans and critical race theory: An examination of school race climate. *Equity and Excellence in Education, 35*(2), 144–154.

Tobias, S. (1993). *Overcoming math anxiety.* New York, NY: W. W. Norton.

Xie, Y., & Shauman, K. (2003). *Women in science: Career processes and outcomes.* Cambridge, MA: Harvard University Press.

Ziliak, S. T., & McCloskey, D. (2011). *The cult of statistical significance: How the standard error costs us jobs, justice, and lives.* Ann Arbor: University of Michigan Press.

HEATHER E. METCALF is a higher education researcher, grant writer, and proposal and award coordinator for the College of Engineering at the University of Arizona.

8

The author provides a framework to help scholars in the field of higher education to be critical. Additionally, the author reflects and comments on the chapters included in this special volume. Finally, this chapter ends with a discussion of the opportunities and challenges of critical quantitative inquiry.

The Changing Context of Critical Quantitative Inquiry

Cecilia Rios-Aguilar

A few years ago, in 2007, Frances Stage edited a volume on critical quantitative inquiry to demonstrate the way quantitative researchers (like many of us) can use their skills to answer critical questions in higher education research. A very important characteristic of critical quantitative scholars, emphasized by all authors, is their ability to challenge the status quo by reframing research questions and challenging concepts, measures, and processes. In this brief commentary, I argue that the context of critical quantitative inquiry focused on educational equity in higher education has changed in the last decade requiring researchers to rethink and reimagine their scholarship. We now must conduct critical scholarship in the midst of more complex contexts: New technologies and ways of communication have emerged, and more interdisciplinary methodologies and conceptual frameworks have been developed. Also, equity-minded researchers in higher education are pressured to produce timely scholarship that is not only rigorous and multidisciplinary but also meaningful and relevant for policy and practice. The main point I want to make in this chapter is that, indeed, the research questions quantitative criticalists ask matter, but the way they go about answering these, the theories they use to interpret findings, and what they do with the findings matter too.

My goal in this chapter is to provide a complementary framework to, hopefully, help other scholars in the field of higher education (whether quantitative or not) to be critical. The framework I discuss here is heavily informed by the scholarship of other criticalists who have impacted various fields (and my own research) in a profound way: Estela Bensimon, Sara Goldrick-Rab, Erin Leahey, and Frances Stage. After presenting the framework, I proceed to reflect and comment on each of the chapters presented

NEW DIRECTIONS FOR INSTITUTIONAL RESEARCH, no. 158 © 2014 Wiley Periodicals, Inc.
Published online in Wiley Online Library (wileyonlinelibrary.com) • DOI: 10.1002/ir.20048

Figure 8.1. Quantitative Critical Inquiry

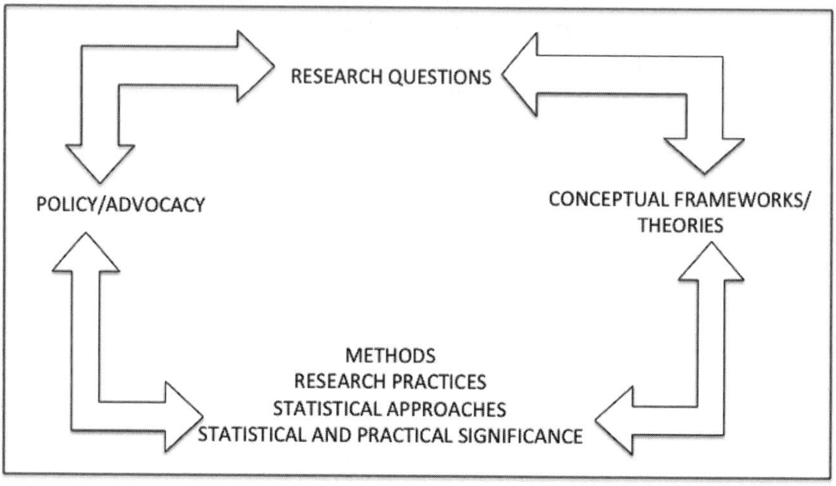

in this volume. I offer insights into what the authors accomplished and also discuss concrete ways in which they, or others, can continue challenging the current state of higher education research.

A Complementary Framework to Think About Critical Quantitative Inquiry

The framework I propose is based on the premise that the interplay between research questions, theory, method/research practices, and policy/advocacy makes quantitative criticalists' scholarship relevant and meaningful (see Figure 8.1). Most of the available literature on this topic (see Stage [2007] and Bensimon & Bishop [2012] for examples of critical research in higher education) has encouraged scholars to think carefully about the research questions they pose. This is still an important task. However, other factors also need to be considered when conducting critical research, particularly quantitative-oriented research. Specifically, higher education scholars need to more closely examine their research practices and the factors that influence these practices. Furthermore, they need to be more intentional about the uses of their scholarship to advocate for equal opportunities for all students.

Conducting quantitative research is a human activity, not immune to social influences (Leahey, 2008). As stated by Leahey (2008), perhaps because of the inherent risks of studying issues too close to one's self, only a small (but increasing) fraction of social scientists have studied social research practices—the decisions that social scientists make as they go about their research. Actually, quantitative researchers are rarely asked to engage in a methodological self-reflection to learn more about why they do the type of research they do, and how they can do it better. This self-reflection, as Breiger (2002) argues, is the only way to allow scholars to recognize the subtleties of practice, which are often burdened with confusion. For instance, a more open discussion of the decisions made, drawbacks, and surprises while scholars do research is certainly needed if we aspire to conduct research that matters in producing equitable opportunities for all students. As Staw (1981) articulates, there is need to investigate the "underbelly of social research—those thoughts, actions, constraints, and choices that lurk beneath the surface of our well-dressed research publications" (p. 225). This improved and continuous dialogue may also contribute to breaking some of the false and unnecessary dichotomies (e.g., having social capital versus not having it) and circular thoughts (e.g., educationally successful groups of students are assumed to possess sufficient quantities of social capital by virtue of their success, whereas underrepresented and nonexcelling groups are assumed to lack social capital and would only do better academically if they acquired it) that plague our research and that continue to perpetuate inequities. In sum, I argue that methodological self-reflection is a key element of quantitative critical inquiry that aspires to improve the lives of millions of underrepresented and marginalized students (and their families and communities).

Leahey (2008) reviewed in detail the many different social influences on various research practices in which sociologists engage in. Concretely, she found that belonging to certain organizations (e.g., departments and/or disciplines) increased the likelihood of the use of certain statistical analyses (i.e., statistical testing). In addition to more traditional organizations, the "methodological communities" that scholars are affiliated with also exert an influence in the way they conduct research (Platt, 1996). Societal norms and individual expectations also play a key role in the way we think of our own work (Leahey, 2008). She argues that scholars constantly take the position of a generalized other to assess their own research: "How is my work going to be received? Is it even publishable?" (p. 41). Finally, Leahey (2008) claims that researchers' assessments of what counts as "valid," "standard," or "rigorous" [and I would add "critical"] methods affect their research approach.

After reading and reflecting on Leahey's (2008) work, I felt the need to know more about the research practices of critical quantitative scholars in higher education. Sadly, we know very little about these. The scant evidence we have shows that higher education scholars need to pay closer attention to the models and statistical techniques they choose to predict several outcomes (e.g., college completion, community college transfer, etc.), particularly when studying underrepresented students. From the brief review we conducted on the research practices of scholars who use multilevel models (see Cheslock & Rios-Aguilar [2008] for details on this review), we learned that methodological sophistication does not automatically lead to more rigorous research nor to better and more relevant results. In fact, we found that, too often, higher education scholars do not justify the need to use a multilevel model. That is, scholars simply estimate a "fancy" model without thinking if this is the best way to answer the research questions posed. Similarly, scholars in higher education claim that using multilevel models leads to a better estimation in standard errors presented by hierarchically nested data, but rarely noted the power of multilevel modeling techniques to control for observed and unobserved level-2 variables, which can yield a better estimation of the magnitude of the coefficients under investigation (Cheslock & Rios-Aguilar, 2011). Likewise, researchers in higher education rarely utilize multilevel models to disaggregate their analyses by estimating level-1 coefficients for a specific group even if the number of observations for that group is relatively small (Cheslock & Rios-Aguilar, 2011).

Multilevel models are not the only case in which a considerable gap often exists between the methods that are recommended in the statistical research literature and the techniques that are actually adopted by applied researchers. Improvements in statistical procedures occur on a regular basis. Indeed, the recent past has witnessed an outburst in the development of methods such as growth curve modeling, propensity score matching, instrumental variables, and regression discontinuity. Interestingly, no study or review has considered the implications of the application of these methods among less methodologically intensive researchers, such as institutional researchers. In other words, existing research does not problematize the fact that institutional researchers may be constrained in a number of ways in applying such sophisticated methods. In fact, institutional researchers face many different challenges with respect to their methodological preferences and choices: (a) time frame, (b) institutional context, (c) level of complexity, (d) relevance to various stakeholders, and (e) effectiveness in communicating findings. The literature has rarely recognized these different needs, and few outlets exist for institutional researchers to obtain critical, simple, and powerful methods that fit their needs. As a result, much research suffers from an ineffective application of complex methods, limited knowledge of applicable methods, and a noncritical perspective.

Another way that future critical quantitative scholars can advance this field is not only by asking research questions that intentionally look at the educational experiences and trajectories of underrepresented groups of students but also by engaging in a self-reflection of the actual research practices and statistical approaches (i.e., choice of centering approach, type of model estimated, number of control variables, etc.) they use and the various influences that affect those practices. But most importantly, critical quantitative scholars must ask themselves how can these multilevel techniques (and many other statistical approaches) be used to unmask inequities.

The work of Mayhew and Simonoff (in press) is an example of utilizing regression analyses with a critical eye. Concretely, they propose the use of *effect coding* rather than *reference coding* when comparing the outcomes of different racial/ethnic groups. Effect coding allows the comparison in out-comes of interest of groups to the grand mean, whereas reference coding compares groups of students with each other, thus allowing scholars to bet-ter understand the outcomes of certain groups of students compared to an institutional average expected for all students, rather than simply compar-ing underrepresented students to the outcomes of White students (Mayhew & Simonoff, in press). By doing so, researchers can avoid silencing the ex-periences of underrepresented students. Furthermore, it will help scholars to stop privileging the backgrounds and experiences of White students.

Another great example of quantitative scholarship that engages in self-reflection is the work of Ziliak and McCloskey (2008). Their recent book, *The Cult of Statistical Significance: How the Standard Error Costs Us Jobs, Jus-tice, and Lives*, shows how economists (and scientists in many other disci-plines) suffer from an obsession with statistical significance. Furthermore, they argue that the quest for statistical significance permeating social sci-ence today is a deeply flawed substitute for thoughtful (and I would add critical) analyses. The lesson, the authors argue, is that significance does not mean important and nonsignificant does not mean unimportant. Thus, it is critical to consider both statistical significance and potential effect size to assess what studies actually show. Furthermore, I suggest critical schol-ars need to discuss the educational significance of their findings. That is, they must engage in a dialogue about what coefficients and effect sizes mean practically for underrepresented and marginalized groups of students' experiences and opportunities. The big questions we need to keep asking are: How are findings informing policy efforts to reduce inequities? How can we incorporate in our scholarship the already existing knowledge and resources that underrepresented students bring to classrooms and higher education institutions? What can institutions and institutional agents do to better support underrepresented students' educational and occupational trajectories?

Furthermore, in addition to a critical examination of research practices related to the methods and statistical approaches utilized, critical quantita-tive scholars also need to pay close attention to the theories and conceptual frameworks used to guide their selection of variables and the interpretation of results, particularly when examining the educational outcomes and tra-jectories of underrepresented students. Some of the available scholarship in higher education, in my opinion, has relied (and continues to rely) on conceptual frameworks that do not capture the precollege and college expe-riences of underrepresented students. Furthermore, we keep neglecting the experiences of many marginalized groups of students (e.g., undocumented students, LGBQT students, foster care youth, and youth in the school-to-prison pipeline). As argued by Bensimon (2007), the scholarship in higher education has "imagined" (Moll, 2000) what students (and I would add their families and communities) need to have and to do to be success-ful based on what dominant models have found to be important factors associated with access to and success in college. Consequently, the existing "politics of representation" (Holquist, 1983) or what Bensimon (2007) labels as the "Tintonian Dynasty" have not resulted in increased completion rates among underrepresented students (Rios-Aguilar & Kiyama, 2012). Consequently, we need alternative models that better capture the actual experiences and circumstances of many groups of underrepresented students.

The scholarship of Estela Bensimon (and colleagues) is an example of research that utilizes asset-based conceptual frameworks (e.g., the funds of knowledge held by practitioners who work closely with college students) to examine equity issues in higher education. Most recently, Bensimon and Bishop (2012) reminded us that the critical study of race in higher education involves an examination of the systematic, tangible and intangible, institutional practices, traditions, and values that operate in various contexts to perpetuate inequities. This concretely means that we must stop blaming students (and their families and communities) for what they lack (e.g., various forms of social and cultural capitals) and, instead, examine both (a) how institutional agents, policies, and practices operate to facilitate (or impede) students' success and (b) how students (and their families) navigate their educational goals and interests in between and in spite of structural constraints (including those imposed by *perpetuating* agents[1]).

Similarly, Sara Goldrick-Rab (and colleagues) has urged researchers to produce theory-driven research that contributes to our understanding of how and why financial aid affects student behaviors and outcomes, particularly those of low-income and underrepresented students. She argues that existing knowledge gaps in the financial aid process are, partly, due to "insufficient theorizing" (Goldrick-Rab, Harris, & Trostel, 2009, p. 3). Goldrick-Rab et al. (2009) introduce several new concepts drawn from various social sciences—aversion to losses, ambiguity, the strength and weaknesses of social ties, work centrality, and the social meanings of money—which might explain other types of financial and life decisions, and therefore, may contribute to elucidate and improve upon the limitations in existing theories (including but not limited to human capital theory, social and cultural capital theories, self-efficacy, and rational choice models). Given that these theories and concepts appear to be valuable in understanding financial and life decisions in other contexts, they also necessitate empirical research in the context of financial aid where numerous unexplained inconsistencies remain (Goldrick-Rab et al., 2009). Not paying attention to these conceptual and empirical issues will continue to perpetuate inequities in higher education.

Finally, quantitative criticalists must ensure that findings of their scholarship are used to change practices and to inform policies. We need to do a better job in translating the results of our sophisticated methodologies into concrete advice for college staff, administrators, faculty, and policy makers. The advocacy activities of scholars such as Sara Goldrick-Rab and Estela Bensimon are excellent examples of what quantitative criticalists must do to improve the quality of life of students, particularly for those underrepresented and marginalized groups. I was particularly impressed by the recent efforts of Goldrick-Rab (and other advocates of financial aid reform) in bringing together scholars, policy makers, and the media to explore opportunities for a more fundamental rethinking of the way financial aid is designed and delivered. At a research conference held in Washington, DC, recently, several researchers presented and discussed concrete innovations in financial aid policy that would create a more effective and sustainable system.[2] From participating in this event, I learned that good (i.e., meaningful, rigorous, and critical) research propels good policy. Therefore, higher education scholars must continue to engage in such advocacy and policy-making efforts.

In summary, the following are the activities in which quantitative criticalists should engage when conducting research:

- Ask relevant questions (about equity and power).
- Choose relevant data.
- Apply appropriate, rigorous, and sophisticated analyses.
- Disaggregate analyses on gender, race/ethnicity, language proficiency, socioeconomic status, and conduct research on several groups of marginalized students (e.g., students who have had contact with the juvenile justice system, indigenous students, and students with disabilities).
- Know how to interpret the results (i.e., pay attention to statistical and educational significance).
- Employ challenging and enriching theories in multiple disciplines.
- Inform and challenge existing institutional practices and decisions.
- Inform and challenge existing educational policies.

A Reflection on This Volume

In this section, I offer some insights from each chapter presented in this special volume. I try to offer a balanced approach by discussing the strengths of each paper and by providing ideas to improve future research on these issues.

Chapter 2: Krystal L. Williams.

Strengths. Williams stressed an imperative need to help practitioners and policy makers understand what interventions work, and how these programs operate for underrepresented students who face a number of challenges and opportunities to succeed in STEM fields. Additionally, the author uses a strength-based approach as an alternative framework to assess efficacy. Most quantitative researchers think theory is not needed. Others think that writing numerous equations count as a theoretical framework. However, equations are no substitute for using theory to critically inform research practices, analyses, and interpretation of findings. Williams reminds

NEW DIRECTIONS FOR INSTITUTIONAL RESEARCH • DOI: 10.1002/ir

us that a conceptual framework is indispensable and must be discussed before methods and findings.

Additionally, Williams includes and justifies variables relevant to underrepresented students' lives. She considers theory when deciding which variables to include in the analyses and how to operationalize them. Both objective and subjective measures are used to better understand the factors that affect underrepresented students' trajectories in STEM fields. Objective measures include the use of public welfare programs, Pell grants, work study, and prior academic challenges as indicated by high school grade point average, and standardized test scores. Students' subjective appraisals of objective barriers include financial stress, ability blame (i.e., contributing academic challenges to lack of ability), and academic discouragement.

Next Steps.   New measures help us understand institutional barriers that impede or facilitate students' success. When using strength-based frameworks, we must remember that focusing on underrepresented students' experiences and decisions is only one piece of the puzzle. Interactions between students' objective and subjective perceptions of barriers *and* concrete institutional practices and policies ultimately influence the efficacy of these interventions. More work is needed using various theories and concepts to operationalize institutional variables (e.g., services provided to students, faculty leadership, and commitment) and program features (e.g., articulation of goals, availability of resources, and funding structure). This type of research would help decision makers and practitioners to design and assess STEM programs that prioritize equity in students' outcomes. Involving institutional researchers in the process of developing these measures is critical not only for improving the validity and reliability of these proxies but also for making the research more valuable and meaningful to decision makers.

Chapter 3: Cynthia M. Alcantar.

Strengths.   Alcantar questions the pragmatism embedded in the "college completion agenda." Alcantar claims that a narrow focus on the role of postsecondary education to improve the economic and global competitiveness of the United States has put human capital and efficiency goals at the top of national agendas. Equity considerations have been forgotten or relegated to a secondary concern. Alcantar's chapter reminds us how important it is to consider not only human capital but also civic engagement for underrepresented students, especially related to academic success.

Another strength of this chapter is the use of the authors' own experiences, usually referred in qualitative research as positionality, to frame the study. Rarely, quantitative researchers are "allowed" or "expected" to articulate their own experiences that help them design studies, use and/or refine theories, select variables, apply statistical techniques, and interpret results. Indeed, all researchers have experiences and perspectives that influence our work; making these explicit can enhance the validity and meaning of our research. This practice needs to be institutionalized in some way for scholars interested in conducting critical quantitative analyses. Finally, this chapter reminds us that we cannot study underrepresented students' civic engagement without understanding the historical and political context of engagement (i.e., social, economic, immigration, and educational policies).

Next Steps.   There is a need for more conceptual and empirical research in this area; it would be helpful to have alternative ways to measure the various types of engagement. This could help researchers who are interested in collecting local data and conducting in-depth research to examine these issues.

Chapter 4: Leticia Oseguera and Jihee Hwang.

Strengths.   Oseguera and Hwang use theories that connect K–12 with postsecondary education. Oakes's framework of critical conditions sheds light on low-income students' educational trajectories by focusing on structural conditions that facilitate or impede students' academic success and does not blame students for their poor academic performance or inability to go to college.

Additionally, Oseguera and Hwang develop figures to depict low-income students' trajectories. The figures are crucial to communicate findings to various audiences. Researchers need to make a better effort to translate complex methodologies and resulting coefficients into something more digestible and useful for educators, policy makers, and the public in general.

Next Steps.   Are there alternative statistical techniques that help us understand low-income students' trajectories? The ELS:2002 data (as well as various other institutional data sets) could be used from a social network approach to examine the structural context proposed by Oakes, Wells, Yonezawa, & Ray (1997). Using transcript data could reveal the ways schools structure opportunity to go to college for groups of underrepresented students. Similarly, institutional researchers can use transcript data to better understand the college trajectories of various groups of underrepresented students and what decision makers can do to make these pathways more equitable. It is important to consider alternative and multidisciplinary theories and methodologies (i.e., social network analysis combined with multilevel models) to better understand structural factors that facilitate or impede students' access to college. Such research will contribute to shifting our perspective from blaming students for lacking intellectual and material resources needed to academically succeed to an approach that pays attention to how educational institutions operate to promote or deny educational opportunities for all students.

Chapter 5: Katherine M. Conway.

Strengths.   Most studies discuss race/ethnicity generally, but not the specific educational needs of millions of immigrant students. Conway provides four concrete examples that illustrate the diverse experiences and resources embedded in immigrants' lives. She specifically disaggregates her analyses based on students' year of arrival to the United States to examine differences in educational experiences and needs of immigrant students. The use of these narratives was important to helping the audience understand the multiple and diverse experiences of immigrant students.

Additionally, Conway reminds us of the importance of "place" when examining the educational trajectories of immigrant students. Failing to better understand how place intersects with educational opportunity perpetuates the idea that only certain places or communities are valuable and worthy of our investments.

Finally, it is crucial to look at the role language plays in immigrant students' educational (and occupational) trajectories, but we need to be careful in how we use labels and how we incorporate them into our analyses. For example, English as a second language (ESL) is a label used only in higher education. Other scholarship (in K–12) has questioned the meaning and value of these labels. Virtually no research in higher education carefully examines the college experiences of English learners. This particular group of students seems to be "lost" once they transition to postsecondary education. Adding a variable to our analyses (e.g., ESL status or language spoken at home) is not enough, thus we need more critical scholarship that uses theory to better understand the experiences and needs of these students. Institutional data sets need to be reexamined and discussed in more detail to determine what other data can be collected to know more about the previous academic and language experiences of students before they enter college and while they attend college.

Next Steps.   Rarely do our quantitative analyses include measures of the broader "context of reception" in which immigrant students "live" particularly in higher education institutions. Immigrant students are often confused with international students in many higher education institutions. Ideally, we would incorporate some aspects of the institutional practices and state policies regarding immigration in our analyses. Being an immigrant student in California is not the same as in Arizona; we must pay closer attention to these various contexts of reception and how they affect students' academic and occupational trajectories. Finally, there is a need to collect more data at the local, state, and national levels regarding immigrant students' educational trajectories. Data must reflect the heterogeneity (e.g., country of origin, undocumented student experiences, students in mixed status homes, etc.) embedded in the various subgroups of immigrant students.

Chapter 6: Ginelle John and Frances K. Stage.

Strengths.   This chapter reinforces the importance of context by focusing on various types of minority-serving institutions (MSIs), the challenges they face, and the successes they have in producing student achievements and accomplishments for students of color earning bachelor's degrees. Much can be learned from the ways these institutions support underrepresented students through to college completion; not enough credit is given to these institutions.

Next Steps. This chapter is useful in highlighting national trends in bachelor degree production among MSIs; however, little research focuses on what these institutions actually do to accomplish this important goal. Are there particular features that make these institutions more effective? Furthermore, there is need to study a broader set of outcomes. Bachelor degree completion is important but also certificate and degree completion, transfer rates, civic engagement, student satisfaction, and employment opportunities for students enrolled in these institutions. Some limitation exists with respect to the availability of data, but that can no longer be an excuse. As mentioned earlier, institutional data sets must be reexamined. There is need to intersect the college experiences of students with multiple institutional contexts to better understand both effective and ineffective programs and practices.

Chapter 7: Heather E. Metcalf.

Strengths. Metcalf reminds us that the STEM pipeline model has been widely utilized to attract underrepresented students to these fields, and to prevent their "leaking" from the pipeline. However, the pipeline model has not contributed to helping us to better understand important power struggles and the multiple educational *and* occupational pathways that many underrepresented students in these fields pursue.

Additionally, Metcalf provides a critical examination of large national data sets: often we see claims from quantitative researchers about the limitations of using secondary data sets. Scholars argue that their inability to provide more nuanced conceptual insights or to utilize better proxies in their analyses is caused by "others" construction of large-scale data sets. Metcalf's research invites us to not be passive users of data sets, but rather use critical lenses to question how these data are constructed, and to raise important equity issues.

She points out the ways some national surveys are designed have consequences for deciding "what counts as science" and "who counts as a scientist and engineer" (p. 90). She found that the educational experiences of students in community colleges seemed to be less valuable than those of students in four-year institutions. Her research highlights the need to examine how identity measures related to race, ethnicity, immigration, and sexuality are constructed and utilized in statistical analyses. This chapter reminds us that the way these measures are created has an impact on a researcher's ability to disaggregate analyses and unmask inequities for certain subgroups of students.

Next Steps. We must continue to conduct more supply side analyses of the STEM pipeline model, while at the same time being critical and paying attention to the fact that the job market in STEM fields may not be as idealistic as some researchers and policy makers have argued. Indeed, recent reports (see Lowell & Salzman, 2007) have found that while there may be more job openings in some areas (e.g., engineering), unemployment rates in others (e.g., computer-related occupations) are persistently high. We must pay attention not only to helping more underrepresented students enter into these fields but also helping them connect with concrete occupational opportunities. Furthermore, it is indispensable to include in our analyses the experiences of students in community colleges who are pursuing degrees or certificates in various STEM fields. Neglecting their experiences and failing to study their educational and occupational pathways in these fields will only perpetuate inequities.

The Changing Context of Critical Quantitative Inquiry

To conclude, scholars and practitioners in higher education must continue finding ways to do more and better critical research. We must start reimagining and reinventing critical quantitative inquiry. To do so, it is imperative that scholars consider new challenges and opportunities. For example, we now must conduct critical scholarship in the midst of new ways of (a) communicating with various *social media* and (b) making decisions with *big data*. We have entered into a new era that calls for more research in higher education that is rigorous, relevant, meaningful, *and* critical.

Notes

1. For more details on a typology of institutional agents see Cruz, Rios-Aguilar, Camacho, and Garcia (2013).
2. For more information about this research conference and the papers presented there, see http://www.aei.org/events/2013/06/24/the-trillion-dollar-question -reinventing-student-financial-aid-for-the-21st-century/.

References

Bensimon, E. M. (2007). The underestimated significance of practitioner knowledge in the scholarship of student success. *The Review of Higher Education, 30*, 441–469.
Bensimon, E. M., & Bishop, R. (2012). Why "critical"? The need for new ways of knowing. In E. M. Bensimon & R. Bishop (Eds.), *The review of higher education: A special issue: Critical perspectives on race and equity* (Vol. 36, No. 1, pp. 1–7). Baltimore, MD: Johns Hopkins University Press.
Breiger, R. (2002). Writing (and quantifying) sociology. In J. Monroe (Ed.), *Writing and revising the disciplines* (pp. 90–112). Ithaca, NY: Cornell University Press.
Cheslock, J., & Rios-Aguilar, C. (2008, November). *Reaping (or not) the benefits of hierarchical data.* Paper presented at the Association for the Study of Higher Education Meeting, Jacksonville, FL.
Cheslock, J., & Rios-Aguilar, C. (2011). Multilevel models in higher education research: A multidisciplinary approach. In J. Smart (Ed.), *Higher education: Handbook of theory and research* (Vol. 26, pp. 85–123). Dordrecht, The Netherlands: Springer.
Cruz, M., Rios-Aguilar, C., Camacho, R., & Garcia, H. (2013, November). *Paving the road to college? The role of institutional agents in shaping the educational and occupational trajectories of Latino males in the school-to-prison pipeline.* Paper presented at the annual conference of the Association for the Study of Higher Education, St. Louis, MO.

Goldrick-Rab, S., Harris, D. N., & Trostel, P. A. (2009). Why financial aid matters (or doesn't) for college success: Toward a new interdisciplinary perspective. In J. C. Smart (Ed.), *Higher education: Handbook of theory and research* (Vol. 24, pp. 1–45). New York, NY: Springer.

Holquist, M. (1983). The politics of representation. *The Quarterly Newsletter of the Laboratory of Comparative Human Cognition, 5*, 2–9.

Leahey, E. (2008). Methodological memes and mores: Toward a sociology of social research. *Annual Review of Sociology, 34*, 33–57.

Lowell, L., & Salzman, H. (2007). *Into the eye of the storm: Assessing the evidence on science and engineering education, quality, and workforce demand.* Washington, DC: The Urban Institute.

Mayhew, M. J., & Simonoff, J. S. (in press). Nonwhite, no more: Effect coding as an alternative to dummy coding with implications for researchers in higher education. *Journal of College Student Development.*

Moll, L. (2000). Inspired by Vygotsky: Ethnographic experiments in education. In C. Lee & P. Smagorinsky (Eds.), *Vygotskian perspectives on literacy research: Constructing meaning through collaborative inquiry* (pp. 256–268). New York, NY: Cambridge University Press.

Oakes, J., Wells, A., Yonezawa, S., & Ray, Y. (1997). Equity lessons from detracking schools. In A. Hargreaves (Ed.), *1997 ASCD yearbook: Rethinking educational change with heart and mind* (pp. 92–110). Alexandria, VA: Association of Supervision and Curriculum Development.

Platt, J. (1996). *A history of sociological research methods in the United States.* Cambridge, UK: Cambridge University Press.

Rios-Aguilar, C., & Kiyama, J. (2012). Funds of knowledge: A proposed approach to study Latina(o) students' transition to college. *Journal of Latinos and Education, 11*(1), 2–16.

Stage, F. (2007). Asking critical questions using quantitative data. In F. K. Stage (Ed.), *New Directions for Institutional Research: No. 133. Using quantitative data to answer critical questions* (pp. 5–16). San Francisco, CA: Jossey-Bass.

Staw, B. (1981). Some judgments on the judgment calls approach. *American Behavioral Scientist, 25*, 225–232.

Ziliak, T., & McCloskey, D. (2008). *The cult of statistical significance: How the standard error costs us jobs, justice, and lives.* Ann Arbor: University of Michigan Press.

CECILIA RIOS-AGUILAR *is an associate professor at Claremont Graduate University.*

INDEX

OTHER TITLES AVAILABLE IN THE
NEW DIRECTIONS FOR INSTITUTIONAL RESEARCH SERIES
John F. Ryan, Editor-in-Chief
Gloria Crisp, Associate Editor

solid starting point for those new to benchmarking in higher education and provides examples of current best practices and prospective new directions. ISBN: 978-1-1186-0883-8

IR 155 **Refining the Focus on Faculty Diversity in Postsecondary Institutions**
Yonghong Jade Xu
Faculty diversity is gaining unprecedented emphasis in the mission of colleges and universities, and institutional researchers are being pushed for relevant data. In this volume, six chapters examine faculty diversity from a variety of perspectives. Together, they constitute a comprehensive outlook on the subject, highlighting factors including racial background, gender, citizenship, employment status, and academic discipline, and examining how growing diversity has affected the work experience and productivity of faculty and the learning outcomes of students. Special attention is given to international and nontenure-track faculty members, two groups that have experienced rapid growth in recent years. Chapter authors present empirical evidence to support the increasing importance of faculty diversity in institutional research, to show the need for actively tracking the changes in diversity over time, and to highlight the critical role of research methodology in all such work.
ISBN: 978-1-1185-2675-0

IR 154 **Multilevel Modeling Techniques and Applications in Institutional Research**
Joe L. Lott, II, and James S. Antony
Multilevel modeling is an increasingly popular multivariate technique that is widely applied in the social sciences. Increasingly, institutional research (IR) practitioners are making instructional decisions based on results from their multivariate analyses, which often come from nested data that lend themselves to multilevel modeling techniques. As colleges and universities continue to face mounting pressures to shrink their budgets and maximize resources while at the same time maintaining and even increasing their institutional profiles, data-driven decision making will be critical. Multilevel modeling is one tool that will lead to more efficient estimates and enhance understanding of complex relationships.
   The express purpose of this volume of *New Directions for Institutional Research* is to illustrate both the theoretical underpinnings and practical applications of multilevel modeling in IR. Chapters in this volume introduce the fundamental concepts of multilevel modeling techniques in both a conceptual and technical manner. Authors provide a range of examples of nested models that are based on linear and categorical outcomes, and then offer important suggestions about presenting results of multilevel models through charts and graphs.
ISBN: 978-1-1184-4400-9

IR 153 **Data Use in the Community College**
Christopher M. Mullin, Trudy Bers, and Linda Serra Hagedorn
American community colleges represent a true success story. With their multiple missions, they have provided access and opportunity to millions of students who would not have otherwise had the opportunity to gain a college degree, certificate, or technical training. But community colleges are held accountable for their services and must be able to show that they are indeed serving their variety of students appropriately. Providing that evidence is the

responsibility of the institutional research office, which must function not only as the data collection point but also as the decipherer of the story the different types of data tell.

This volume speaks of the multiplicity of data required to tell the community college story. The authors explore and detail how various sources—workforce data, market data, state-level data, federal data, and, of course, institutional data such as transcript files—all have something to say about the life of a community college. Much like an orchestral score, where the different parts played by individual instruments become music under the hands of a conductor, these data can be coordinated and assembled into a message that answers questions of student success and institutional effectiveness.

ISBN: 978-1-1183-8807-5

IR 152   **Attracting and Retaining Women in STEM**
Joy Gaston Gayles
Underrepresentation of women in science, technology, engineering, and mathematics fields is a problem that has persisted over the past three decades and is most severe at the highest levels of the STEM career path. Although national attention has been directed toward increasing the presence of women in STEM, women continue to leave at critical junctures in STEM training and careers at a higher rate than men. This volume of *New Directions for Institutional Research* takes a comprehensive look at the status of women in STEM and considers related factors, theoretical perspectives, and innovative tools that have the potential to help scholars understand, study, and improve the experiences of women in STEM fields.

ISBN: 978-1-1182-9769-8

IR 151   **Using Mixed-Methods Approaches to Study Intersectionality in Higher Education**
Kimberly A. Griffin, Samuel D. Museus
This volume of *New Directions for Institutional Research* focuses on using mixed-methods approaches and intersectionality frameworks in higher education research. The authors draw on intersectionality as a foundational theory for framing questions and interpreting results and discuss the importance of using a variety of methods to get useful, deep, honest answers from college faculty and students. They provide several examples of how such broad perspectives enhance the quality of scholarly and institutional research on faculty experiences and relationships, the challenges faced by faculty of color, college access and equity, privilege in higher education, campus climate research and assessment, and multiracial college students' experiences.

ISBN: 978-1-1181-7347-3

NEW DIRECTIONS FOR INSTITUTIONAL RESEARCH

ORDER FORM SUBSCRIPTION AND SINGLE ISSUES

DISCOUNTED BACK ISSUES:

Use this form to receive 20% off all back issues of *New Directions for Institutional Research*.
All single issues priced at **$23.20** (normally $29.00)

TITLE	ISSUE NO.	ISBN

*Call 888-378-2537 or see mailing instructions below. When calling, mention the promotional code JBNND
to receive your discount. For a complete list of issues, please visit www.josseybass.com/go/ndir*

SUBSCRIPTIONS: (1 YEAR, 4 ISSUES)

☐ New Order   ☐ Renewal

U.S.	☐ Individual: $89	☐ Institutional: $317
CANADA/MEXICO	☐ Individual: $89	☐ Institutional: $357
ALL OTHERS	☐ Individual: $113	☐ Institutional: $391

Call 888-378-2537 or see mailing and pricing instructions below.
Online subscriptions are available at www.onlinelibrary.wiley.com

ORDER TOTALS:

Issue / Subscription Amount: $ _____

Shipping Amount: $ _____
(for single issues only – subscription prices include shipping)

Total Amount: $ _____

SHIPPING CHARGES:
First Item $6.00
Each Add'l Item $2.00

*(No sales tax for U.S. subscriptions. Canadian residents, add GST for subscription orders. Individual rate subscriptions must
be paid by personal check or credit card. Individual rate subscriptions may not be resold as library copies.)*

BILLING & SHIPPING INFORMATION:

☐ **PAYMENT ENCLOSED:** *(U.S. check or money order only. All payments must be in U.S. dollars.)*

☐ **CREDIT CARD:** ☐VISA ☐MC ☐AMEX

Card number _____Exp. Date_____

Card Holder Name_____Card Issue # _____

Signature _____Day Phone_____

☐ **BILL ME:** *(U.S. institutional orders only. Purchase order required.)*

Purchase order # _____
Federal Tax ID 13559302 • GST 89102-8052

Name_____

Address_____

Phone_____ E-mail_____

Copy or detach page and send to: **John Wiley & Sons, One Montgomery Street, Suite 1200,
San Francisco, CA 94104-4594**

Order Form can also be faxed to: **888-481-2665**

PROMO JBNND

Great Resources for Higher Education Professionals

tudent Affairs Today

2 issues for $225 (print) / $180 (e)

et innovative best practices
r student affairs plus lawsuit
ummaries to keep your institution
ut of legal trouble. It's packed
ith advice on offering effective
ervices, assessing and funding
rograms, and meeting legal
equirements.

udentaffairstodaynewsletter.com

Campus Legal Advisor

12 issues for $210 (print) / $170 (e)

From complying with the ADA
and keeping residence halls
safe to protecting the privacy of
student information, this monthly
publication delivers proven
strategies to address the tough
legal issues you face on campus.

campuslegaladvisor.com

Campus Security Report

12 issues for $210 (print) / $170 (e)

A publication that helps you
effectively manage the challenges
in keeping your campus, students,
and employees safe. From
protecting students on campus
after dark to interpreting the latest
laws and regulations, *Campus
Security Report* has answers
you need.

campussecurityreport.com

ational Teaching & Learning Forum

issues for $65 (print or e)

om big concepts to practical details and from
utting-edge techniques to established wisdom,
TLF is your resource for cross-disciplinary discourse
student learning. With it, you'll gain insights into
arning theory, classroom management, lesson
anning, scholarly publishing, team teaching,
nline learning, pedagogical innovation, technology,
nd more.

lf.com

Disability Compliance for Higher Education

12 issues for $230 (print) / $185 (e)

This publication combines interpretation of disability
laws with practical implementation strategies to help
you accommodate students and staff with disabilities.
It offers data collection strategies, intervention models
for difficult students, service review techniques,
and more.

disabilitycomplianceforhighereducation.com

ean & Provost

2 issues for $225 (print) / $180 (e)

om budgeting to faculty tenure and from distance
arning to labor relations, *Dean & Provost* gives
u innovative ways to manage the challenges of
ading your institution. Learn how to best use limited
sources, safeguard your institution from frivolous
wsuits, and more.

eanandprovost.com

Enrollment Management Report

12 issues for $230 (print) / $185 (e)

Find out which enrollment strategies are working
for your colleagues, which aren't, and why. This
publication gives you practical guidance on all
aspects—including records, registration, recruitment,
orientation, admissions, retention, and more.

enrollmentmanagementreport.com

WANT TO SUBSCRIBE?
Go online or call: 888.378.2537.

JB JOSSEY-BASS™
A Wiley Brand